ADVANCING
RACIAL LITERACIES in
TEACHER EDUCATION

ADVANCING RACIAL LITERACIES in TEACHER EDUCATION

ACTIVISM
FOR EQUITY
IN DIGITAL SPACES

Detra Price-Dennis
Yolanda Sealey-Ruiz

Foreword by Jabari Mahiri
Afterword by Rebecca Rogers

TEACHERS COLLEGE PRESS
TEACHERS COLLEGE | COLUMBIA UNIVERSITY
NEW YORK AND LONDON

Published by Teachers College Press,® 1234 Amsterdam Avenue, New York, NY 10027

Library of Congress Cataloging-in-Publication Data is available at loc.gov

ISBN 978-0-8077-6550-0 (paper)
ISBN 978-0-8077-6551-7 (hardcover)
ISBN 978-0-8077-7964-4 (ebook)

Printed on acid-free paper
Manufactured in the United States of America

This book is dedicated to our children: Ashlee, Brandon, Olivia, and Wynter. Thank you for inspiring us to keep searching for ways to make schools worthy of your brilliance.

Contents

New Racial Literacies in the Digital Age

At the dawn of the third decade of the 21st century, we still grapple with how to prepare and support educators to meet challenges of teaching and learning in the digital age. In 2020, virtual reality spawned words like "blursday," "doomscrolling," and "Covidiot," while old words like "lockdown" and "elbow-bump" also expressed our new reality. Along with the pandemic, other perilous societal challenges became more acute, such as climate crisis, extreme poverty and income disparities, and myriad racial inequities. These grave problems are intricately linked, and their impacts are further magnified through the lens of race.

Teachers College professors Detra Price-Dennis and Yolanda Sealey-Ruiz have developed a bifocal lens on racial and digital literacies that seamlessly integrates theory and practice with cogent arguments and compelling examples from their research of multiple ways for *advancing racial literacies in teacher education*, particularly regarding crucially needed *activism for equity in digital spaces*. This definitive book convincingly reveals the necessity of centering race and digital literacies in K–12 classrooms by enacting racial literacy in teacher preparation and practices.

Three tenets of racial literacy—questioning assumptions, critical conversations, and reflexivity—are key to evidence- and fact-based meaning-making processes and progressive actions by teachers and students to ameliorate the dynamics of race and racism. Importantly, these tenets, joined with the incisive concept of the "archaeology of the self," also are needed to understand and effectively address other divisive societal issues that turn on the axis of race, especially in the digital age where misinformation and disinformation are rampant.

For example, results of a December 2020 NPR/Ipsos poll of 1,114 U.S. adults indicated that 40% said they believe the coronavirus was made in a lab in China, although scientists have confirmed that it was transmitted to humans from another species. Two-thirds of Republicans surveyed said they believed that voter fraud was the reason Joe Biden won the presidential election, despite any evidence supporting this claim and more than 60 court cases rebuking it. Another belief by 47% of respondents was that the majority of racial protests during the summer of 2020 were violent. Instead, they were overwhelmingly peaceful. The pollsters felt that multiple factors made people susceptible to misinformation, including educational attainment, media consumption, and, importantly, the likelihood to believe perspectives that fit into their worldviews. In each example, racialized perceptions about Blacks and violence, about Blacks and voting, or about Chinese people were central misperceptions upon which erroneous beliefs and assumptions were based.

In U.S. schools, where the vast majority of teachers do not share racial, ethnic, linguistic, and cultural backgrounds with their students, critical conversations and reflexivity about race can be distressing for teachers and students alike. That is why this book's systematic ways of guiding educators and students through iterative stages of institutionalizing racial and digital literacies are so potent. It provides definitions of key terms connected to race and racism. It anchors the origins of "racial literacy" in the work of feminist sociologist France Winndance Twine, then links it to critical race theory through the legal scholarship of Lani Guinier. It illuminates the significance of the Black Lives Matter movement and the international struggles it has inspired to advancing racial literacies. Essentially, this work argues not only for the power but also the liberation inherent in personally and collectively questioning racial assumptions—the old racial literacies—and revising them to take action toward righting the wrongs of race. For me, this constitutes *new* racial literacies.

Ultimately, this work questions assumptions that underlie the very "idea" of race. The authors indicate that race is not a scientific fact, yet engage it as a social fact with devasting consequences for those at the bottom of racial hierarchies. They illustrate how digital tools deepen racial hierarchies and increase social control. Questioning these hierarchies undoubtedly leads to understanding how they have been perpetuated by the ideology and institutions of White supremacy, in part through a historically propagated White/Black binary with other color-coded categories capriciously placed between the poles.

In questioning these hierarchies, teachers and students necessarily come to terms with the complexity of their identities—generationally, geographically, and across the spectrum of gendered positionalities. Archaeologies of the self will take each person back in time and space to ancestral antecedents that reveal more authentic individual and group identities. For those identified as White, these may be places where they did not have that identity prior to successive waves of White expansion in the United States that over time incorporated Irish, Polish, Italian, German, Jewish, and other people into Whiteness.

Deeper understanding of racial identity and diversity reflect conceptual change; greater movement toward racial equity and affinity require behavioral change. *Advancing Racial Literacies in Teacher Education* significantly contributes to the conceptual and behavioral changes needed for teachers and students to realize a transformative idea of race.

—Jabari Mahiri

Introduction

As I was walking down the hall of a suburban middle school, I saw a small group of Black female students talking near the entrance. I greeted them and continued toward the office. After a few steps in the opposite direction, I heard one of them say, "She must be a substitute. We don't ever have no Black teachers in this building. It's not fair." I stopped, well, more like I froze. I felt the weight of their words and the tenor of their frustration grounding me to the space where I was standing. I remember having those same thoughts and sense and frustration that I heard in their voices.

(Research Journal, Detra)

EXPLORING RACE IN TEACHER EDUCATION

It has been widely documented that the majority of teachers in our school systems do not share the same racial, cultural, ethnic, or linguistic background with the students they teach (Brown, 2014; Evans-Winters & Twyman Hoff, 2011; National Center for Education Statistics, 2013; Sleeter, 2017). It is evident from the vignette above, as well as from recent studies (Haddix, 2012; Martinez, 2017; Tatum, 1997), that students are aware of this "cultural gap" and are becoming increasingly frustrated with systems that espouse a rhetoric of diversity, while failing to hire teachers who mirror their racial, cultural, and linguistic practices. Our experience in teacher education has shown that conversations about race in teacher education happen infrequently and with great trepidation (Sealey-Ruiz, 2013; Skerrett, 2011). Very few studies provide insight into how teacher educators mediate conversations about race (Haddix & Price-Dennis, 2013; Lyiscott, 2017; Rogers & Mosley, 2006); how they do so using digital tools (Price-Dennis, 2016); ways that they support their preservice teachers' interrogation of race and its impact on schooling (Greene & Abt-Perkins, 2003; Michael, 2014; Price-Dennis & Souto-Manning, 2011); and how they create opportunities for students to take up

1

racialized issues as part of their teaching in the field (Milner, 2006; Price-Dennis, Fowler-Amato, & Wiebe, 2014; Sealey-Ruiz & Greene, 2015). A goal for this book is to provide a theoretical foundation that offers practical insights into how to address issues of race and equity as they unfold in the digital age in teacher education.

Three days after Detra overheard the above exchange, she shared it with a group of preservice teachers during their weekly seminar. She asked them to discuss their recommendations for how the staff in that school could respond to the students' observations about the lack of Black teachers. The majority of the preservice teachers indicated they did not believe the teachers in that school were responsible for the situation and, therefore, they should stay out of it. They did not believe that school was a place to bring in politics, especially about race and affirmative action. A few preservice teachers in the class disagreed and suggested that the staff at the school meet with the students to develop a statement about diversity and hiring that could be shared with the board of education. However, the few students who made this suggestion also shared that they would be concerned if this were to happen at their school because they did not feel prepared to talk about race with their students or colleagues.

The discussion revealed a serious conundrum, as well as several insights, about this group of future teachers:

1. The majority of them were using highly politicized ideas as a means to argue for neutrality in public education.
2. The majority of them did not see themselves as educators who were responsible for advocating for their students, especially when it involved race.
3. The majority of them viewed race as a negative political construct rooted in deficit ideology.
4. The preservice education program still had a lot of work to do to support the racial literacy development of novice teachers.
5. None of the preservice teachers seemed aware that middle school students spend time talking about issues of race and how race impacts their educational experience.

Although this exchange took place several years ago, it is still applicable to the current sociopolitical context of education we navigate each day.

Racial and digital literacies have the potential to equip teachers with skills and perspectives that allow them to grow, learn, live, and thrive in a society that needs an approach to teaching and learning grounded in humanizing ways of being and knowing. We draw on both of these bodies of work to expand on previous scholarship that foregrounds equity, social justice, multicultural education, and culturally responsive pedagogy/culturally relevant pedagogy. In this book, we define racial literacy as a skill and practice with which individuals are able to probe the existence of racism and examine the harmful effects of racial stereotypes. A desired outcome of racial literacy in a historically racist society like America is for members of the dominant racial category to adopt an antiracist stance and for persons of color to resist a victim stance. We draw on Lankshear and Knobel's (2008) work and define digital literacies as "myriad social practices and conceptions of engaging in meaning making mediated by texts that are produced, received, distributed, exchanged via digital codification" (p. 5). The development of racial literacies in the digital age can help teachers speak against racial injustice, in particular, and encourage their students to do so through technological means that simultaneously encourage them to reimagine a world where equity in education is tied to civic engagement in digital spaces.

EXPLORING RACE IN THE DIGITAL AGE

We are currently grappling with the crippling effects of a global pandemic. In early 2020, the COVID-19 virus hit the United States and many countries in Europe and Asia in a seemingly sudden and most certainly devastating manner. Within weeks after the virus began to claim lives, American schools shifted to remote education. What once lingered in the shadows—widespread online learning, MOOCs, webinars, and hybrid classes—suddenly became the method of how we teach and the way we learn. The virus exposed what we always knew to be true—there is a deep digital divide (Prieger & Hu, 2008) and existing inequalities that become exacerbated in a time of crisis. To the surprise of very few, race and racism were at the root of it all. Innovative scholars like Ruha Benjamin (2019) have made clear arguments in their work about how racism in our society is reflected and manifested through the use of technology. Benjamin's work specifically acquaints us with how digital tools deepen racial hierarchies and are used in pernicious ways to increase social control, particularly of those in communities who have been marginalized by the social construction of race. As COVID-19 raged through Black and Brown communities, causing a record number of deaths (Kendi, 2020), it also brought a heightened awareness of the "digital divide" in schools that predominantly serve Black and Brown children. We witnessed how school districts, like ours in New York City, scrambled to make technology for remote learning accessible to students. We witnessed the sudden impact of how children of various abilities, linguistic backgrounds, and academic levels were left struggling as a result of their unequal access to digital tools (Barnwell, 2020).

If the devastation brought by the onslaught of the COVID-19 virus were not enough to endure, we as a nation were already experiencing an intense upswing in the fight for the well-being and rights of immigrants, women, and people of color. In 1966, 3 years after the historic March on Washington, in an interview with CBS correspondent Mike Wallace, Reverend Dr. Martin Luther King Jr. said, "I think that we've got to see that a riot is the language of the unheard. And, what is it that America has failed to hear? It has failed to hear that the economic plight of the Negro poor has worsened over the last few years." Protests, or expressions of what King called "the language of the unheard," are a way that marginalized groups resist infractions on their civil rights; they are how the disenfranchised seek and build coalitions with others in person and online. For example, #BlackLivesMatter (#BLM), #TakeaKnee, #Metoo, #Charlottesville, #Portland, and #Kenosha all are resistance movements that either began with a social media campaign or are sustained by one. These examples illustrate why teacher educators should engage their students with racial literacy in today's times, mainly because these teacher education students—and, without doubt, their own future students—are members of online spaces. In understanding the learning needs of students in the 21st century (and in this time of remote learning), teachers will recognize that these young men and women will continue to be educated through online platforms, even when COVID-19 ends. As a result, they may be influenced to join online and in-person uprisings because they or members of their family have been affected by racial injustice.

In this book, we argue that there are multiple affordances of privileging racial and digital literacies in teacher education. We explore the sociotechnical spaces that are pushing and driving the social agenda around race and education, profoundly impacting how we design our teacher education courses. We believe that teacher education programs should adopt some of the powerful hashtag syllabi that scholars who study race have already created. For example, aspects of the #BLM movement have inspired a curriculum (blacklivesmatteratschool.com) and a syllabus (Roberts, 2016) that can be featured in teacher education program courses to both teach about the movement and engage teacher education students with literacy around digital activism. The #BLM movement offers a potentially powerful model of what happens when we interweave racial and digital literacies. To begin unpacking this issue, the field will need teachers who are:

1. prepared and have the skills to talk about difficult and sensitive issues in the classroom;
2. able to move beyond their own biases in order to reimagine the work they are called to do; and
3. ready to navigate how to develop curricula and pedagogy informed by skill and reflexive practice in person and in digital spaces.

WHY DO WE NEED TO CENTER RACE AND DIGITAL LITERACIES IN K–12 CLASSROOMS?

This is an unsettling time in U.S. history where teacher educators, as well as other public interest professions, are witnessing unprecedented moments of uncertainty. The election results of 2016 ushered in massive challenges to democratic ideals. Racism, sexism, xenophobia, homophobia, and anti-immigrant sentiments are reflected in the national discourse in a manner that supports marginalization and dehumanization of minoritized populations. This is evident in the uptick of hate crimes, gun violence, acts of terrorism motivated by racism, and the murdering of coconspirators in the movement for racial justice—like Heather Heyer, a White woman killed by an anti-#BLM protestor in 2017 in Charlottesville, Virginia.

SAY THEIR NAMES

Since 2017, and up to the moment this book went to press, dozens of Black people[1] have been murdered by the police across the nation.

---

1. **2020:** Ahmaud Arbery, Jacob Blake, Marcellis Stinnette, Jonathan Dwayne Price, Dijon Durand Kizzee, Rayshard Brooks, Carlos Carson, David McAtee, Tony "Tony the Tiger" McDade, George Perry Floyd, Dreasjon "Sean" Reed, Michael Brent Ramos, Daniel T. Prude, Breonna Taylor, Manuel "Mannie" Elijah Ellis, William Howard Green; **2019:** John Elliott Neville, Atatiana Koquice Jefferson, Elijah McClain, Ronald Greene, Sterling Lapree Higgins; **2018:** Emantic "EJ" Fitzgerald Bradford Jr., DeEbony Groves, Charles "Chop" Roundtree Jr., Chinedu Okobi, Botham Shem Jean, Antwon Rose Jr., Saheed Vassell, Stephon Alonzo Clark; **2017:** Aaron Bailey, Charleena Chavon Lyles, Fetus of Charleena Chavon Lyles (14–15 weeks), Jordan Edwards, and Chad Robertson.

Some of the deaths made more prominent by the media include George Perry Floyd in Minneapolis, Minnesota (2020); Ahmaud Arbery in Glynn County, Georgia (2020); Breonna Taylor in Louisville, Kentucky (2020); Jacob Blake in Kenosha, Wisconsin (2020); DeEbony Groves in Nashville, Tennessee (2018); and Botham Jean in Dallas, Texas. These murders, along with steady racial profiling of Black Americans leading to police involvement for everyday things like barbecuing in a park or taking a nap in a college dorm, remind Americans of a not-too-distant past when Confederate flags were flown and giant crosses were burned in expression of centuries-old racial hatred for Black American citizens. Lessons from history teach us that these events do not occur in a vacuum and have an impact on how children and families navigate issues of race in their communities, especially in their schools.

As a society, we have also watched social protest movements unfold in real time via social media. In turn, many of us have become voyeurs as well as active participants acclimated to the idea of digital activism—with social media being used to publicize and develop political movements that expose systemic racism and racial violence. We are teaching and learning in a time where digital spaces have transformed the method by which citizens protest and speak back to the social injustices they witness in society. Reflective of past movements for justice, students are now at the forefront of these activist literacy practices (#Parkland; #SanteFe; #1000Blackgirlbooks; #IStandwithAhmed; #NationalSchoolWalkout; #blackinbrooklyntech), thereby merging social action with social media in school spaces. Given that students are already centering digital ways of knowing as a means of addressing social issues, developing racial literacies in teacher education is necessary to support preservice and classroom teachers as they learn to: (a) navigate sociotechnical spaces with a critical lens; (b) develop strategies that support their students' ability to discuss issues of race in sociotechnical spaces; and (c) interrupt harmful narratives that circulate in digital spaces, but impact face-to-face interactions in school. It is our hope that this book will increase teachers' capacity and agency to organize and respond to inequities that plague our educational system.

PURPOSE OF THE BOOK

Throughout this book, we have made a conscious effort to merge theory and practice. We recognize that the majority of frameworks that address racial and cultural inequity in schools are presented in a siloed manner. However, we seek to create an interdisciplinary conversation that centers race in teaching and learning in a digitally driven world. We believe racial literacy provides one lens for viewing the effects race has on the daily lives of teachers and students. This is not meant to diminish the effects of other constructs, but to foreground the realities of living in a racialized society. As such, we designed this book to build capacity for racial literacy in teacher education by providing a framework that invites the reader to rethink how curricula and pedagogy impact classroom instruction.

KEY TERMS

Some key terms are used or referred to throughout this book. We lean on the extensive literature in various fields and theories—from sociology to psychology, and from new literacy studies to critical race theory—to understand and operationalize the term *race* as having not a biological basis, but rather a social construction with a pernicious and violent history attached to it that significantly impacts how people, and specifically BIPOC (Black, Indigenous, and People of Color), experience their lives. We also recognize that even as certain people and policies are in favor of the idea of privileging Whiteness, we ascribe to the notion that race is fluid, complex, and ever changing. We view the term *literacy* as an expansive concept involving social, cultural, and academic practices. In the case of *racial and digital literacies* per se, we understand these to be skills that are developed, with competencies displayed to show what has been taught and learned. We understand *racism* to be an ideologically and socially supported system of privileges in favor of White people, who have been scripted to be "more human" than others. It is institutionalized by discriminatory practices at the federal, state, and local levels that impact collective and individual perceptions about the "races" in our society. In relation to education, many who lead school systems, as well as teachers and teacher education students in colleges and universities, refuse to believe that racism is a major influencer for how children experience and perform in school. We understand *stereotypes* to be widely accepted, oversimplified descriptions or images of people. We recognize *bias* as an inclination to act against an individual or group based on assumptions, prejudgments, and stereotypes, and *discrimination* as the act of judging and then withholding opportunity or resources from an individual or a group based on a perceived characteristic. We understand *prejudice* as a prejudgment of an individual or a group based on a bias, stereotype, or preconceived notion. The *archaeology of self* is central to Yolanda's racial literacy development model. It is a theoretical concept and practice that asks individuals to excavate biases, stereotypes, and prejudicial beliefs that are held within. We recognize *activism*, particularly as it relates to Black and Brown children, to be actions that are taken to bring a condition or policy more in alignment with humanity for all children, and to dismantle the unequal and unjust ways BIPOC and other marginalized children are treated in society.

ORGANIZATION OF THE BOOK

In Chapter 1, *Engaging and Embracing Racial Literacy in Teacher Education*, we provide a survey of the educational landscape in relation to racial literacy, including culturally responsive pedagogy, culturally relevant pedagogy, and culturally sustaining pedagogy. We draw on our scholarship in this area to provide examples of how racial literacy can be fostered in teacher education. Toward the end of the chapter, we present a series of reflection questions designed to guide readers in assessing the status of race in their programs and in K–12 education.

In Chapter 2, *How Can Racial Literacy Inform Teacher Education in the Digital Age?*, we explore the potential for racial literacy to inform the ways teacher preparation programs can prepare their students to develop curricula and pedagogies that encompass digital literacies. This chapter provides insights into how the construct of race circulates in digital spaces to help us reimagine how to develop a curriculum that leverages multimodal ways of cultivating racial literacy. It also presents a framework for taking up racial literacies and digital literacies in teacher education: Racial Literacy for Activism (#RL4A). It concludes by drawing our attention to how teacher education can take up the framework to advance racial literacy across technologies toward meaningful change.

In Chapter 3, *Institutionalizing Racial Literacy in Teacher Education*, we advance the notion of racial literacy as a culturally sustaining practice that should be institutionalized in teacher education. It provides examples of racial literacy in action within a teacher education program and in a high school classroom, and discusses the three tenets of racial literacy development that are necessary when engaging topics of racism, race, and other interlocking identities toward a fuller understanding of how the construction of race manifests in educational spaces.

Chapter 4, *Engaging in Critical Multimodal Curation to Foster Racial Literacy*, focuses on a pedagogical practice that supports the principles of Racial Literacy for Activism (#RL4A) in action across educational contexts. Specifically, this chapter highlights learning experiences aligned with multimodality that examine racism through the collection and organization of artifacts designed, created, and curated by students.

The concluding Afterword is by Dr. Rebecca Rogers, a leading scholar in the field of racial literacy. The unifying intent throughout the book is to provide information about racial literacy in the digital age that encourages and inspires teachers to rethink how curricula and pedagogy impact classroom instruction. We are excited to begin this journey with you. As you read and raise questions or examples of how you are enacting the Racial Literacy for Activism framework, feel free to share your thoughts and work samples using the hashtag #RL4A.

CHAPTER 1

Engaging and Embracing Racial Literacy in Teacher Education

Racism is a profound neurosis that nobody examines for what it is.

Toni Morrison (1992)

The year is 1955. A 14-year-old Black teen from Chicago visits his family. In the sweltering Mississippi summer heat, Emmett Till walks with his friends to a convenience store where he comes into contact with 21-year-old Carolyn Bryant Donham, the daughter of the store owners. Carolyn accuses Emmett of grabbing her and making sexual advances toward her. Within a few days he is hunted down, taken from his great-uncle's home in the middle of the night, beaten, shot in the head, tied to a cast-iron fan, and thrown into the Tallahatchie River. After a massive hunt, Emmett's body is pulled from the river. Emmett's killers—Carolyn's husband and another White man—are brought to trial and exonerated by an all-White jury. Shortly after they are declared innocent, the men admit to killing Emmett. Their confession is published in *Look*, a national magazine. Although they go public with their confession, they cannot be tried twice for the same crime. Sixty years later, on her deathbed, Carolyn admits to a journalist that Emmett was innocent this whole time.

In November 2018, a story hit the pages of a national magazine that 26-year-old Kristen Rimes of Columbia, South Carolina, lied to the police and filed a false report stating that she was attacked and "almost" sexually assaulted by a Black man. Kristen is a White woman.

In December 2018, a video of a toddler and her mother went viral on Instagram. Within a few days, the post of a mother "interrogating" her daughter about who ate the box of Ms. Kipling's cakes received nearly three million views. Following her mother's line of questioning, the little girl insists that someone broke into their home and stole the pastries. As the mother questions her, the little girl squirms in her chair and sheepishly looks all around the room. When she finally speaks, she tells her mother it was a Black man who broke into their home and stole the pastries. The mother responds with uproarious laughter, and the toddler, relieved that she has successfully gotten herself out of trouble, laughs along with her mother. The toddler and her mom are White.

A peek into history reveals countless stories of Black men being false-ly accused of assaulting White women. From the Scottsboro Boys in 1931 to George Stinney Jr. in 1944 to the examples listed above, the insidious trope of Black men harassing and hurting White women is one that is etched into the American psyche. Racism lies at the center of a history from which Americans try to run, but it is persistent be-cause it is passed down to newer generations with very little interrup-tion and many variations.

In *Stamped From the Beginning: The Definitive History of Racist Ideas in America*, Ibram X. Kendi (2016) traces history to solidify the argu-ment that it has *always been about race*. Black people, from the very conception of the American "democracy," were "stamped" to be less than human. To help move the development of an American demo-cratic nation forward, entrepreneurial slaveholders fortified the exclu-sion of Blacks from humanity and politicians codified it through laws and policies. Enslaved Black bodies were the necessary ingredient in America's recipe for capitalist gain, freedom from Britain, and power. Kendi's book makes a compelling argument that racist ideas did not arise from ignorance or solely from the hatred of Blacks, but from a devised plan of exclusion—designating Blacks as subhuman to justify the American system of slavery, and the deeply entrenched discrimi-natory laws, policies, and practices that followed to keep Blacks from access to education, good health, wealth, and freedom.

The fact is that as long as Black people have been in this country, their struggle has never ceased. Historically and currently, Black peo-ple are embroiled in a perennial fight for fair treatment, justice, and a decent education. Some of the most noted philosophers and edu-cators have theorized the role education plays in determining social success and well-being. The Children's Defense Fund and Freedom Schools founder Marian Wright Edelman reminds us that education is a necessity in order to survive in America today. Those of us who study history know that the challenge of Black people to receive a decent education traces back to the design of their role in this nation to be chattel slaves. The intention was never for Black people to be educated; therefore, it should come as no surprise that some of the more consistent battlefields in the fight for equity happen on school grounds and in academic spaces. It should not be surprising that many Black academics have dedicated their research careers to the topic of educational equity and issues of inequality involving race. We choose to dedicate our academic lives to these issues because we desire to do all that is within our reach to improve educational opportunities for Blacks and other children who are marginalized because of their race and social location. We seek to fully test the spirit of America's democracy and the power of education to change lives in that democracy.

Our challenge as American citizens is to decide if race will continue to serve as a deterrent to opportunity for some, or act as a catalyst toward advancing a world where pluralism and diversity can be realized once and for all. From school integration battles to conflicts on the use of the N-word, all aspects of our society can benefit from the concept of racial literacy. Racial literacy offers an opportunity to move us closer to open and honest dialogue that can potentially shift the way we think about race, move hearts and minds, and spur the creation of policy that serves all of humanity.

The concept of race is deeply rooted in our lives and is articulated through our legal, financial, health, and education systems, to name a few. Race affects how we think, speak, and perform culture. Although an abundance of research shows that race is not real—meaning it is not biological but is socially constructed (Omi & Winant, 1986) and must be deconstructed (Mahiri, 2017)—Frankenberg (1993) argued that "race, like gender, is 'real' in the sense that it has real, though changing, effects in the world, and real, tangible, and complex impact on individuals' sense of self, experiences, and life chances" (p. 11). Developing the racial literacy of educators is critical to helping them succeed and read the racialized world in which they live (Freire, 1974). If educators are able to engage in these critical conversations, then they are better equipped to resist the rampant racist practices that disproportionately impact students of color. Racial literacy in teacher education, for example, can go against the ways that colleges and universities perpetuate the status quo of White domination through curricula that normalize Whiteness and discourage open and critical conversation about race and racism (Churchill, 1995; Schick, 2002). In education writ large—and in teacher education specifically—there is limited theorizing around racial literacy development (Bolgatz, 2005; Johnson, 2009; Rogers & Mosley, 2006; Skerrett, 2011). While the concept is gaining traction in education (Mahiri, 2017; Stevenson, 2014), those who are becoming familiar with the idea consistently ask two questions:

1. What *exactly* is racial literacy?
2. Why is it important that we develop racial literacy in educational settings?

WHAT IS RACIAL LITERACY?

Racial literacy is a concept developed by sociologist and feminist researcher France Winndance Twine (2003, 2010). Twine's research in the United Kingdom with English and Irish women who were members of interracial families (mothers of children fathered by Black men) revealed a form of racial socialization in which these parents engaged to help protect and defend their children against racism. Racism is a structural phenomenon that determines one's status and opportunity in society. This determination is often influenced by the color of one's skin and the racial category ascribed to that color. Racism is the belief that one race is superior to another. In the United States and other racially stratified societies, racism is supported by the legal system and codified through societal and cultural practices. It is characterized by acts of discrimination against, as well as prejudice and antagonism toward, members of a marginalized racial category (Mahiri, 2017), while members of the situatedly dominant category are centered. Twine (2003, 2010) advances the notion that racial literacy is enacted through strategies and practices that are linked to culture and heritage. This approach requires that racial injustice (in action and words) must also be responded to with action and words in order to counter racism effectively. What Twine found significant in her research to countering racism for African-descendant children was the use of aesthetic and material resources that promote the intelligence, creativity, and significance of Black culture across the diaspora, including the United States.

Racial literacy is an ideology prominent in the fields of sociology and legal studies; in recent times, it is also being closely examined in the field of education (Bolgatz, 2005; Mahiri, 2017; Rogers & Mosley, 2006; Sealey-Ruiz, 2011; Sealey-Ruiz & Greene, 2015; Skerrett, 2011; Stevenson, 2014). Racial literacy is a skill practiced when individuals are able to probe the existence of racism and examine the effects of race as it intersects with institutionalized systems. Individuals with racial literacy are able to articulate their experiences and representation in society. As applied to teaching and learning in schools, racial literacy is the ability of students to identify, in professionally published and student-generated texts, concepts related to race and racism, and exercise their skills in discussing the complexity of these topics. For example, they investigate how race and racism manifest in the lives of the characters they read about and they are able to make comparisons to their own lives. Students who have this skill are able to discuss the constructions and implications of race, specifically American racism, in constructive and forward-thinking ways. A desired outcome of racial literacy in an outwardly racist society like America is for members of the dominant racial category to adopt an antiracist stance and for persons of color to resist a victim stance. Racially literate students reflect on their experiences with race and are reflexive about their attitudes and beliefs. They write and read texts that are meant to elucidate their understanding of race and racism and equip them with language to talk about these concepts (Sealey-Ruiz & Greene, 2011).

The ever-increasing diversity of our classrooms and our world makes a strong case for racial literacy education. The concept of racial literacy is informed by scholarship that recognizes race as a signifier that is discursively constructed through language (Hall, 1997); fluid, unstable, and socially constructed (Omi & Winant, 1986) rather than static; and not rooted in biology, but as Frankenberg (1993) wrote, having "real" effects in the lives of individuals. Race is a socially constructed ideology, and racism is the system that upholds and perpetuates that ideology, which results in material outcomes for people's lives. Racism is a system of oppression that is pervasive, restrictive, and hierarchal (Adams et al., 2007). Racism functions "not only through overt, conscious prejudice and discrimination but also through the unconscious attitudes and behaviors of a society that presumes an unacknowledged but pervasive white cultural norm" (p. 6). Thus, through this lack of acknowledgment, racism creates and maintains the "invisible" dominant power structure. Mahiri (2017) argued for a *new kind* of racial literacy, one where we must move beyond racial categories that are defined by a capitalistic, White-dominated world. Instead, he argued, we must make space to discuss and understand the nuances of race and how it intersects with various interlocking identities and the world of the digital—which offers vast possibilities to create new, interesting, and complex identities. Mahiri urged all of us to move toward an articulation of race that is in line with the 21st century's ever-evolving categories of race, which are fluid and multicultural.

The concept of racial literacy gained prominence in legal studies with Lani Guinier's 2004 article "From Racial Liberalism to Racial Literacy: *Brown v. Board of Education* and the Interest-Divergence Dilemma" published in *The Journal of American History*. In this article, Guinier demanded a shift from racial liberalism to racial literacy. She critiqued racial liberalism as an inactive, deficit approach to racial equality that subjugates Blacks to the position of victim and does not activate the required antiracist stance that Whites must take against their own racist ideals and actions. We focus on the *Brown v. Board of Education* case in the next few paragraphs because having an understanding of the most infamous educational equity case in history helps to contextualize some of the modern-day struggles we witness in educating all children, particularly Black children in today's schools.

RACIAL LITERACY AND *BROWN V. BOARD OF EDUCATION*

In his research and public talks, Khalil G. Muhammad—professor, scholar of African American history, and activist—argued for the need for American citizens to attain historical literacy to better understand ourselves as a nation (Moyers, 2016). He asserted the instrumentality of historical literacy in helping to determine how we move forward as a country, specifically as it pertains to race. We concur with Muhammad and endorse the idea that before racial literacy can be effectively built and practiced, citizens—and, most specifically, citizen educators—must build their historical literacy. Knowledge of the past has a direct and significant connection to understanding present-day racial crises, especially for those of us who work in the field of education.

The most well-known case regarding the impact of race on educational opportunity is *Brown v. Board of Education of Topeka, Kansas*. The decision delivered by Chief Justice Earl Warren in 1954 stated that school segregation, as it was examined in the five cases[1] that made up *Brown v. Board of Education*, was unconstitutional and a violation of the Fourteenth Amendment. The responses to this landmark decision by academics and legal strategists, and most specifically opinions

---

1. Delaware: *Belton v. Gebhart* (*Bulah v. Gebhart*); Kansas: *Brown v. Board of Education of Topeka, Kansas*; Washington, DC: *Bolling v. Sharpe*; South Carolina: *Briggs v. Elliott*; and Virginia: *Davis v. County School Board of Prince Edward County*.

expressed by Guinier (2004), who brought the term *racial literacy* to the legal world, are important to examine for both historical and political insights into the state of education for Black children in the United States. In her article, Guinier argued that as a society we must move beyond symbolic models of racial "progress" like *Brown v. Board of Education* and move toward becoming a racially literate society. In agreement with Guinier, scholars of racial literacy suggest that as a society we must engage a more nuanced understanding of how deeply embedded the concept of race is in our society, how it maintains the status quo of racial hierarchy, and how it impacts every aspect of our lived experiences.

With the hindsight of more than half a century since *Brown v. Board of Education* (1954), it is obvious that the promise of racial and educational equality associated with the landmark case has fallen short of expectations (Bell, 1980, 1983, 2002; Guinier, 2004; Orfield, 1988). Among the retrospective reflections on the case's legacy is the sober contention that while *Brown* is an important icon in the nation's constitutional canon, in its configuration as a "bench-based, lawyer-crafted social justice initiative" (Guinier, 2004, p. 97), the legal effort was, at best, a well-intentioned but ill-equipped decision intended to address the complex set of social, political, and economic problems that make up the matrix of race-related educational inequality, and at its worst, a failure in moving the nation forward in the struggle for equity.

There is a distinction to be made between Twine's (2003) concept of racial literacy and the term *racial literacy* as theorized by Guinier (2004). While Twine was focused more on the individual's need to survive and thrive in a racist society, Guinier advocated that a paradigm shift from racial liberalism to racial literacy is needed because racial liberalism only proved to uphold the system of White supremacy and did not enact much change for Black people. Guinier argued that the actual power in support of educational equity behind *Brown v. Board of Education* was very weak and limited. The pivot of the case was not "the intentional coalescing of a transforming social movement that reached across boundaries of race and economic class, but . . . the calculated convergence of interests between northern liberals, southern moderates, and blacks" (p. 94). It is this convergence of interests that Bell (1980) argued helped to shape the legal strategy advanced by *Brown*'s advocates. Guinier (2004) outlined how, in developing the case for formal desegregation, the plaintiff's legal team brandished a thesis that sought to emphasize, from a psychological point of view, the deleterious impact that segregation had on the psyche of Black children. In doing so, the lawyers sought to encourage the court to address the psychological damage Black children endured and interrupt the intangible effects of stigma and self-hate. This "intangible damage thesis," Guinier argued, was seen as the best possible route to building wide consensus around the case. As the case occurred in a "court-centered universe," the goal of desegregation became the *ultimate goal,* which, Guinier argued, mistakenly shifted the focus away from true educational equity.

By centering segregation's psychological damage on Black children, integration became the focal point of the argument in *Brown v. Board of Education* and desegregation became the ultimate goal. Equality became redefined, "not as a fair and just redistribution of resources, but as the absence of formal, legal barriers that separated the races" (p. 95). In *Silent Covenants:* Brown v. Board of Education *and the Unfulfilled Hopes for Racial Reform*, Bell (2004) wrote, "*Brown*, in retrospect, was a serious disappointment, but if we can learn the lessons it did not intend to teach, it will not go down as a defeat" (p. 193). As Guinier eloquently argued, *Brown v. Board of Education* spotlighted the psychological damage that segregation enacted toward Black people without attending to the psychological benefits that Whiteness and segregation conferred on White people. Further, the case relegated to relative obscurity the relationship between inequality and other factors, such as resource distribution.

While *Brown v. Board of Education* was couched in the interest convergence between northern liberals and southern moderates, and Blacks, Guinier argued, it "perpetuated a more durable divergence of interests within and between black and white communities" and "did little to disrupt the historic pattern in which race was used to manufacture dissensus . . . within and outside communities of color" (p. 113). She offered this definition for racial literacy, seemingly the most hopeful approach to getting people to disrupt the historic pattern of racism:

> Racial literacy is an interactive process in which race functions as a tool of diagnosis, feedback and assessment. Second, racial literacy emphasizes the relationship between race and power. Racial literacy reads race in its psychological, interpersonal and structural dimensions. It acknowledges the importance of individual agency but refuses to lose sight of institutional and environmental forces that both shape and reflect that agency. (p. 115)

In various ways, then, even as *Brown v. Board of Education* brandished the aspiration for racial and educational equality, it did not—perhaps could not—attend to the complex ways in which race codes, cloaks, and normalizes racialized hierarchies. Over 65 years after the landmark decision, we are face-to-face with an education discourse on race that requires skill for a complex analysis.

THE ELEPHANT IN THE ROOM: RACIAL LITERACY IN SCHOOLS

Howard C. Stevenson (2014), author of *Promoting Racial Literacy in Schools: Differences That Make a Difference*, deepened our understanding of racial literacy and took up what Toni Morrison mentioned during her Charlie Rose interview: Racism is a mental disease that, for the most part, has gone unexamined. Stevenson's work can be seen as a response to Morrison's quote, a way of taking up her invitation to examine the psychological impact of racism on those who perpetuate racist acts and those who are on the receiving end of negative racial encounters. According to Stevenson, racial self-efficacy and literacy are defined "as the belief in and ability to read, recast, and resolve racially stressful encounters" (p. 19). His work with Black families revealed the power of storytelling in developing racial literacy and healing racial wounds (L. A. Bell, 2010). Stevenson's research showed that immediate relief comes with storytelling, but emphasized that making known one's reality by sharing stories about lived experiences is the beginning of the lifetime work involved in building and sustaining racial literacy and in healing the heart and mind when racist incidents happen:

> While mastering the basic literacy skills of racial self-observation could take a lifetime, another benefit of storytelling is seeing racial stress in others. Becoming facile at appraising one's stress reactions during racial encounters teaches individuals to notice the stress reactions of other people. More important, one can become competent at choosing to respond to those reactions differently. Seeing racial stress in others makes them more predictable and perhaps less threatening. (p. 17)

The cover of Stevenson's book has a pink elephant running through a school hallway. Many, if not most, of us have heard the discussion of race referred to as the "elephant in the room"—the one thing everyone sees because of the space it takes up, but no one wants to acknowledge actually exists. Acknowledging the "elephant" for White people often means they have to interrogate their privilege, face the guilt that comes with unfair skin color advantage, and listen to why Indigenous, Black, Latinx, and Asian people are often so frustrated with White people and the systematic structures that secure and ensure their advantage over others. For people of color, and Black people in particular, facing the "elephant in the room" is dealing with the anger they hold toward Whites and the systematic structures that assure the advantages of Whites at the cost of stifling opportunities for others. The "elephant in the room" is also the resentment Blacks feel about what racism has created within them—often self-hate, resentment of their own people, and Black rage—and having to come to terms with the fact that however hard they work, how much they achieve, and how much access they attain, they will never be able to shake their Blackness in a country built on the ideology and idolatry of Whiteness.

Our definition of racial literacy and our approaches to developing it closely align with the arguments of Guinier (consideration of individual and systemic racial politics), Twine (focus on relationships), and Stevenson (recognition of the power of the personal story in understanding the impact of racism). Our definition suggests there are three tenets of racial literacy, which we will describe below, and six components of racial literacy development, which include a need for a critical love; a critical humility; a critical reflection; historical knowledge; a deep examination of the self in relation to racism, bias, and stereotypes; and the moral courage to interrupt racism and inequality when one thinks, hears, or sees them in action. Interruption is an important step toward racial literacy becoming a sustained practice toward change and positive racial relations, particularly in school settings. Racial literacy in schools can be defined as a skill and practice in which students probe the existence of racism and examine the effects of race and other social constructs as they intersect with institutionalized systems that affect their lived experiences and representation in U.S. society. Students with racial literacy are able to discuss the implications of race and American racism in edifying and constructive ways. In short, racial literacy is the ability to examine, discuss, challenge, and take antiracist action in situations that involve acts of racism. Guinier (2004) offered a robust challenge to racial and social justice advocates seeking to deal with the shifting landscape of racial inequalities and called for a racial literacy to engage this work.

WHY RACIAL LITERACY NOW?

In his book *Faces at the Bottom of the Well: The Permanence of Racism*, legal strategist and critical race theorist Derrick Bell (1992/2018) solemnly asserted that racism *has always* been with us and will *continue to be* with us in spite of any progress achieved through social reform. Certainly, in the 25+ years since his book was first published in 1992, problems centering on race in America have all but intensified. More than a decade after the election of Barack H. Obama, the first Black president, America continues to struggle with the concept of freedom and justice for all. This is a critical time in U.S. history where the teaching profession, as well as other public interest professions, is witnessing unprecedented moments of uncertainty. Travel bans, immigrant children taken from their families and locked in cages, ICE (Immigration and Customs Enforcement) raids, and threats of deportation have created confusion and turmoil in the lives of many immigrants who may still hold on to the hope of becoming American citizens.

Notwithstanding these recent challenges for immigrants, Americans are also witnessing threats to the concept of well-being and belonging for some groups in our society. The debate around the Confederate flag and the frustration expressed by many Americans about the toppling of Confederate statues remind us of a not-too-distant past when Confederate flags were flown and giant crosses burned to express a deep-seated and centuries-old racial hatred for Black American citizens. That hatred, in recent decades, has erupted in dozens of killings of unarmed Black men, women, and children by the police; shootings in synagogues, churches, schools, and movie theaters—places where people go to pray, learn, and relax—sending the message that no place is safe, and any one of us at any time can be the victim of a hate crime. Racial literacy is sorely needed to assist police officers in examining their beliefs about Black people and other citizens who have been marginalized and are the subject of targeted bias. Racial literacy is also needed for teachers to acquire and practice a language that probes how bias and anti-Blackness manifest as trauma and crisis in the lives of students at school. When students are not invited to talk about their feelings associated with racial tragedies that happen in their neighborhood or society writ large, and when there is a paucity of caring, concerned, and informed adults who are equipped with the skills to have these conversations, then students are deprived of an opportunity to process their feelings and pain (which is necessary for healing). In addition, they are not provided the opportunity to learn about structural racism and ways to interrupt the bias they have against others. Knowledge about structural racism and the other interlocking oppressions that impact their lives is an important aspect of students' successful navigation of structural racism. They cannot navigate what they do not know exists, nor can they interrupt what is not talked about and examined.

More than ever before, there is a need to not just talk about race and racism, but to learn how to examine carefully how race is lived in our society. As teachers and adults in the lives of children, we must develop and display the personal moral courage to alter the outcomes of racism. We have the power to make change and transform mindsets, even as we do our work in a society and an educational system that both create and perpetuate racial inequality. Making a difference starts with us. Making a difference starts with developing our own racial literacy and inviting and encouraging the development of racial literacy in others. We live in an era that feels eerily familiar for some of us, where Blacks have to state that their lives matter, and people who do not neatly fit into categories that have been constructed as "normal" and "mainstream" find themselves protesting for basic rights and humane treatment. The violence we witness daily is violence that impacts all of us, particularly the children we teach. In July 2016, as a response to the murders of two Black men by police—one in Louisiana and one in Minnesota—and the killings of five police officers in Dallas, former New York City Chancellor Carmen Fariña sent an open letter to families and colleagues in New York City. In her letter, Fariña (2016) wrote:

> As painful as these events are, I strongly believe that as New York City educators and parents, we have a moral obligation to address the difficult questions about race, violence, and guns, and to engage students in the critical work of healing our country. We must not avoid these tough conversations—they are necessary if we hope to build a just society for all.

Teachers and students need racial literacy to have these discussions, and schools must be equipped with school staff and leaders who possess the skills to have these important conversations with parents.

THREE TENETS OF RACIAL LITERACY

In schools, healthy conversations on the effects of racism across class, culture, race, and other characteristics of diversity are possible. Multiple texts and modalities to engage students in these conversations are readily available through digital technologies. To develop racial literacy among students, the use of historical, fictional, poetic, and digital texts is most effective. Teachers who are able to engage their students successfully in the topic of race are most effective when they have engaged in self-exploration and honest assessments of their role in perpetuating racist ideas. Once specific behaviors are recognized, it becomes easier for the racially literate person to interrupt those behaviors in future moments and guide others to do the same. Individuals who develop racial literacy are able to engage in necessary personal reflection on their racial beliefs and practices and teach their students and staff to do the same. Racial literacy in schools includes the ability to read, discuss, and write about situations that address racial inequity and racial bias as part of the norm of schooling process.

Utilizing research with teachers and English education students, a move toward racial literacy can be achieved through a new theory called an "Archaeology of the Self" (Sealey-Ruiz, 2020)—the self-exploration, probing, excavation, and understanding of where issues of race, racism, and human phobias live within individuals. Personalizing race and recognizing how individuals perpetuate racism is a first step toward racial literacy. For teachers who develop racial literacy, a natural progression is (re)examination of what and how they are teaching, and a deliberate development of culturally responsive educational approaches in their classroom. Teachers who engage in racial literacy development seek to decolonize their pedagogy and create a foundation for equitable practices in their classroom.

Over a decade, we have observed the enactment of three tenets while working with inservice and preservice teachers as they engage with their beliefs and practices during a racial literacy development process: question assumptions, engage in critical conversations, and practice reflexivity.

Question Assumptions

Fundamental to racial literacy development (see Figure 1.1) is for individuals to question their assumptions about race, acknowledge their biases, and take the stance that much of what they "assume to know" about race is faulty and incomplete. In questioning assumptions about race, individuals take a stance to actively resist and interrupt the racist and discriminatory practices, policies, and beliefs they encounter in their teaching sites.

Engage in Critical Conversations

Engaging in critical conversations is an integral component of racial literacy development. Individuals must be encouraged to work toward, and eventually develop, the confidence to discuss their hesitancies and concerns about teaching in racially diverse settings. The intent of these critical conversations is to focus on language, on how biases and racist attitudes are articulated, sometimes in an unconscious or dysconscious manner. Critical conversations are outlets for actively and openly questioning assumptions that the individual holds about race.

Practice Reflexivity

Reflexivity is a very important process in racial literacy development. It offers the mirror needed to do the important work of identifying where we need to make changes in our lives—work that must be done toward a deeper understanding of the cultural, social, and political influence (Arunasalam, 2017). Reflexivity offers the opportunity to help locate a teacher's position, which influences how we see the world (Crenshaw, 1991). However, there must be a building toward reflexivity. Time must be spent understanding more about the self in relation to racism and racial injustice to make meaning of one's personal journey in this work (Finlay, 2002). Reflexivity in racial literacy development is a cyclical process of (re)examining perceptions, beliefs, and actions relating to race. It is a crucial step in racial literacy development. This promotes the idea of (de)constructing and (re)building a base for new perceptions founded on open-mindedness and understanding that comes from engaging the six components of racial literacy development.

RACIAL LITERACY AS RESISTANCE

Yolanda, a coauthor of this book, has been fortunate to have incredible mentors throughout her life. These were extraordinary individuals who worked toward the "race problem" in America on the big stage. One

Figure 1.1. Racial Literacy Development

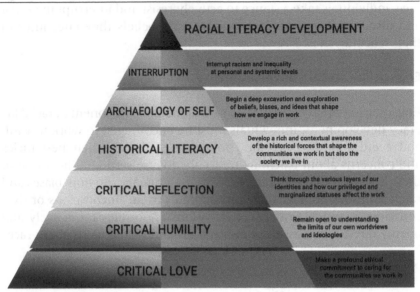

RACIAL LITERACY DEVELOPMENT

INTERRUPTION — Interrupt racism and inequality at personal and systemic levels

ARCHAEOLOGY OF SELF — Begin a deep excavation and exploration of beliefs, biases, and ideas that shape how we engage in work

HISTORICAL LITERACY — Develop a rich and contextual awareness of the historical forces that shape the communities we work in but also the society we live in

CRITICAL REFLECTION — Think through the various layers of our identities and how our privileged and marginalized statuses affect the work

CRITICAL HUMILITY — Remain open to understanding the limits of our own worldviews and ideologies

CRITICAL LOVE — Make a profound ethical commitment to caring for the communities we work in

of her mentors was Emmy Award–winning talk show host Gil Noble. For more than 4 decades, Gil hosted *Like It Is*[2] on ABC Channel 7 in New York City. During many of their long telephone conversations, Gil lamented that the "biggest problem" for Black people was gaining the right to sit at the Woolworth counter for lunch and a cup of coffee. Gil believed that once Blacks "earned the right" to sit next to Whites in public, they lost focus on other inequalities that required an intense and sustained fight. Gil also believed, like others (Foster, 1998; Guinier, 2004), that the ultimate goal of school integration did not work in favor of Black people. He felt that the illusion of integration led Blacks to further take their "eyes off the prize"[3] by convincing themselves they had "arrived" once a few of them were able to live in the same communities as Whites and work side by side with them in industry. Gil did not bemoan the successes that Blacks had achieved; after all, he fought and won to have a successful television show on a major network channel

---

2. *Like It Is* was a media platform to express ideas and perspectives—particularly those of Blacks—that were ignored by mainstream news media. Gil Noble hosted the show from 1968 until his death in April 2012.

3. This was an allusion to *Eyes on the Prize*, a 14-part documentary film about Black Americans' fight for their civil rights in America.

for over 40 years. However, he believed that with comfort came a weakening of a rich tradition of protest. Yolanda and Gil often talked about how the idea of protest—even at times when it appeared ineffective and seemingly "begging the White man for what was inherently ours"—had to remain at the forefront for Blacks. Uprisings, he believed, were one of the most effective ways of resisting the lies that Black lives *did not* matter. As Bell (2002) wrote, "Resistance is a powerful motivator precisely because it enables us to fulfill our longing to achieve our goals while letting us boldly recognize and name the obstacles to those achievements" (pp. 171–172). Black people have always been very clear on what stands in the way of their freedom, and they boldly name these obstacles even as they fight against them.

Those who practice racial literacy have a strong historical knowledge of past events and can make connections to current events. Their ability to talk about race and racism in constructive ways can and often does incite their imagination in service of resistance. From kneeling down on football fields, to school district protests over the disproportionality of Blacks in special education, to exposing their under-representation in gifted and talented classes, Black people who have built their racial literacy have resisted the status quo of inequality. Despite their existence in a society that refuses to acknowledge their humanity, there are examples throughout history of how Blacks have resisted degradation and the control of their destinies, and remained creative when their communities were crumbling, neglected, and stereotyped as degenerate. Multiple "movements" in education over the decades have offered educators a way to equip students with historical knowledge that can help them be racially literate and informed about the injustices they witness and experience. Racial literacy continues in the tradition of these movements—it is more than a theoretical concept and an approach for people to engage with history to understand the present. Racial literacy can be seen as part of the "movement" that views educational spaces as grassroots organizing sites that prepare individuals for the "racial battles" they will fight for equity and equality in schools and society.

ARCHAEOLOGY OF THE SELF IN
RACIAL LITERACY DEVELOPMENT

Racial literacy is a skill that allows people to engage in deep conversations about race and other social constructions within which we live. It is the ability to talk productively about race and racism with the intent of moving toward the interruption and dismantling of racist and unequal practices and policies. All of the components of the racial literacy development model are crucial for the progression of racial equity and the dismantling of racist policies and practices; however, it is the individual who is at the center of activating these components. The Archaeology of the Self process is a steady and deep self-excavation where racism, stereotypes, and bias live. One must have generosity with the self in doing this work. Excavation must be done privately, but also in community. The sharing of space in the racial literacy journey helps to push individuals toward publicly declaring their role in the work of interrupting and ultimately dismantling racist beliefs and practices. We are humans sharing space and we are all living under the "smog" of racism (Tatum, 1997). We are influenced by one another toward racist ideology, and it will take each of us to work toward influencing each other in antiracist ways. Tatum (1997) noted:

> To say that is not our fault does not relieve us of responsibility, however. We may not have polluted the air, but we need to take responsibility, along with others for cleaning it up. Each of us needs to look at our own behavior. Am I perpetuating and reinforcing the negative messages so pervasive in our culture, or am I asking to challenge them? If I have not been exposed to positive images of marginalized groups, am I seeking them out, expanding my own knowledge base for myself and my children? Am I acknowledging and examining my own prejudices, my own rigid categorizations of others, thereby minimizing the adverse impact they might have on my interactions with those I have categorized? Unless we engage in these and other conscious acts of reflection and reeducation, we easily repeat the process with our children. We teach what we were taught. The unexamined prejudices of the patterns are passed on to the children. It is not our fault, but it is our responsibility to interrupt this cycle. (p. 86)

It is crucial for individuals to realize how their action or inaction impacts the status quo of inequality, and what that impact exacts on their lives and the lives of others. In *The Fire Next Time*, author and activist James Baldwin (1963) reminded us that no one can escape the ills of White supremacy—not those who identify as White nor Black and Brown people. Indigenous Australian visual artist Lilla Watson reminded us of the collective achievement (Hucks, 2014) that is necessary in the work of liberation: She wrote, "If you have come here to help me, you are wasting your time, but if you can come because your liberation is bound up with mine, then let us work together" (quoted in Rodriguez et al., 2020). Racism stands against love and justice for people of color in America. The Archaeology of the Self work must be done individually *and* in community for it to have the influence and power needed to bring about the dismantling of racism and move toward recognition and respect for the *full* and wonderful humanity of people of color.

FROM ETHNIC STUDIES TO RACIAL LITERACY EDUCATION

In the early 1900s, W. E. B. Du Bois, arguably the father of modern scientific sociology and the first Black man to receive a PhD from Harvard University, insisted on the need to teach Black history in schools. His call sparked the fire that burned decades later during the civil rights movement when student protests against Eurocentric-dominated curricula erupted on college campuses throughout the United States. In fact, it was the 1968 uprising of the Third World Liberation Front, protesting the lack of diversity in curricula, students, and staff at San Francisco State College, that helped to establish ethnic studies as a college major in colleges and universities across the country.

In 1975, almost a decade after the college protests began, scholar James Banks helped to advance the ethnic studies movement with his book *Teaching Strategies for Ethnic Studies.* In 1995, Banks and his wife, Cherry McGee Banks, published the first edition of the *Handbook of Research on Multicultural Education.* The *Handbook* solidified multicultural education as a field of study that should be taken seriously and infused into K–12 schools as well as higher education. By the time the second edition of the *Handbook* was released in 2004, the field of multicultural education had seen the emergence of scholars like Sonia Nieto, Gloria Ladson-Billings, and Geneva Gay—educational theorists who wrote about the significance of multicultural education and forged a new field of study around culturally relevant and responsive K–12 education. Their theories led to the progression of related fields like critical race theory (in education),[4] critical literacies, and, in the mid-2000s, the field of racial literacy. In 2005, Jane Bolgatz published

---

4. Gloria Ladson-Billings and William Tate's (1995) article "Toward a Critical Race Theory of Education" (*Teachers College Record, 97,* 47–68) introduced critical race theory to the field of education. Critical race theory was developed by legal strategists Derrick Bell, Patricia Williams, Richard Delgado, Kimberlé Williams Crenshaw, Camara Phyllis Jones, and Mari Matsuda.

her research as *Talking Race in the Classroom*, which examined the racial literacy of participants of a high school social studies classroom. A year later, in 2006, Rebecca Rogers and Melissa Mosley published the groundbreaking article "Racial Literacy in a Second-Grade Classroom: Critical Race Theory, Whiteness Studies, and Literacy Research," which featured research on racial literacy in an early-grades classroom. In the mid-2010s, the work of Allison Skerrett, who examined the racial literacy of high school English teachers, and LaGarrett King (2016), who investigated the racial literacy of teachers in social studies classrooms, deepened the theory of racial literacy and affirmed its importance in the field of teacher education.

RACIAL LITERACY IN TEACHER EDUCATION

In 2018, it was estimated that of the 51 million students (National Center for Education Statistics [NCES], 2018) in the United States who would attend pre-K through 12th grade, about half (26 million) would be children of color. This level of diversity means that educators must be prepared to support the academic thriving of children from various ethnic backgrounds. If educators are to develop a pedagogy that embraces multiracial, multiethnic, multilingual students, then racial literacy must be developed early in their teaching practice and sustained throughout their career. Learning to genuinely understand and accept their students' multiple ways of knowing and being can fundamentally shift educators' perceptions and challenge stereotypes they may hold about their students and the communities in which they live. This approach requires intense self-work (probing biases, and racist and stereotypical ideas held about students and their families), and the strength to challenge the self and others to embrace a more equitable and just way of life for all students.

Serious work regarding racial literacy development is also needed beyond teacher preparation programs. School leaders must think deeply about the type of professional development they offer their teachers and the opportunities they provide for reflection on their practice. School leaders must also create space to build racial literacy skills by allowing teachers the opportunity, honestly and nonjudgmentally, to discuss their pedagogy with one another and find ways to support and meet the needs of their richly diverse students. Identifying sustainable approaches is a necessity if diverse students are to have full and rewarding schooling experiences. Developing teachers' racial literacy will lay the foundation for them to create culturally relevant/responsive and culturally sustaining pedagogies (Paris & Alim, 2014) that center students' linguistic abilities, cultural practices, and ways of knowing and being in the classroom. In this way, both teachers and students are recognized as knowers.

The development of racial literacy in classrooms is possible when the three tenets of questioning assumptions, engaging in critical conversations, and practicing reflexivity are present. There should also be an explicit and deliberate interdependence in the teaching and learning process between teachers and students, and a mutual understanding of what is at stake—the liberation of minds and hearts from racist ideology. The quest for racial literacy in classrooms then becomes a collaboration between teachers and students—a collaboration in understanding lived experiences, fears, desires, and hopes for a better classroom experience as well as understanding everyone's individual roles in creating a better world. Teacher and student agency is centered in a racially literate classroom. In classrooms such as these, creative, political, and divergent thinking lays the groundwork for better student outcomes and open spaces to speak for students who are often silenced and positioned marginally in the educative process. Without a shared responsibility for a more just and humane world, the onus falls on teachers to create spaces in which students are, at best, passive recipients of what is offered; such spaces are unlikely to disrupt racism when students see or experience it.

Racial literacy building includes conversations that promote the examination of cultural identities in the classroom and work toward social justice. Racial literacy should be viewed as a way to bolster culturally relevant/responsive and culturally sustaining pedagogies in our schools in order to develop an understanding around challenging issues and lessen the chasm between teachers and students. Race, as well as the many other social constructions (gender, class, religion) we live with and within, affect student outcomes and student–teacher relationships. Classrooms that nurture racial literacy in both students and teachers offer a fertile ground for these pedagogies to become common practice and to flourish.

Racial literacy urges educators to take a close look at an institutionalized system like school and examine it for the ways in which its structure affects students of color. Educators who develop racial literacy are able to discuss the implications of race and racism in constructive ways that can transform their teaching. They develop an ability to resist labeling students as "at-risk" based on race and social status and are more likely to view racialized students as "at-promise"—those who need and deserve increased educational opportunities (Milner, 2010). Clearly, the significance of this discourse is not small.

This book argues that there is a dire need for racial literacy in teacher education. As salient as race is to our lives, it remains a topic that needs constant (re)examination, which must be done in context. Teacher educators must seek to understand how race affects pedagogy in classrooms and schools and how it impacts the discourse of diverse communities and societies, and then teach this to their students. Admittedly, this pedagogical approach is emotionally and politically charged and laden with challenges (Guerrero, 2008; Isaksen, 2008; Kim, 2008; Mangino, 2008). However, we ask: How can possessing racial literacy help to build coalitions in schools and reduce prejudice and racial bias, and impact the teaching and learning process in a way that serves all children?

Perhaps now more than ever, developing racial literacy in teacher education has the potential to help teachers build capacity and agency to organize and respond to inequities that plague our educational system. Race and racism are subjects that teachers and teacher educators are often uncomfortable discussing. Engaging such subjects in a constructive manner requires the application of racial literacy. Teachers and students with racial literacy are able to discuss the implications of race and American racism in edifying ways. We do not mean to imply that race is the only salient issue affecting our society; however, race and racism, and their corollaries—White domination and privilege—are institutionally supported in education. This, among other issues, leads to the (mis)labeling of students and to negative impacts on their achievement. Those who engage their racial literacy must do so with the intent to foster open dialogue about race, and issues pertaining to race (ethnicity, language, sexual orientation, etc.), with the goal of liberating their students. Preservice teachers, like all adult learners, come into learning situations with ideas, knowledge, beliefs, and values constructed from their life experiences. Often when preservice teachers enter their teacher education programs, they do so with preconceived notions about their future career and students; these notions are often informed by persistent stereotypes cemented through the media (Sealey-Ruiz & Greene, 2015).

It is challenging to help educators unravel these stereotypes and misperceptions about students, schools, and teaching because everyone has *some* experience with school. For example, preservice teachers have been students for most of their lives; therefore, they believe they have some understanding of what goes on in classrooms. Often, if they have had negative experiences with teachers and fellow students, they bring these experiences with them as "factual evidence" of what happens in schools. Therefore, for them, teaching and learning often carries problematic and unexamined assumptions, beliefs, and "knowledge" about teaching, learning, and students. These assumptions are not always well examined or made explicit while they are earning their certificate or degree (Carrington & Selva, 2010; Hollingsworth, 1989), yet they have a profound effect on their future decisionmaking and classroom practices (Hollingsworth, 1989). Thus, what preservice educators bring with them when they enter their teacher education programs can and does have great implications for the learning experiences of their future students.

Teacher educators who seek to build the racial literacy of their students should be asking: Can our classrooms be places where we can challenge our minds and hearts? Can we focus our teacher education programs on disseminating knowledge that promotes equity? Should teachers serve (and develop their students) as vanguards and enforcers of equity? Building racial literacy as a practice in preservice teacher education strives to reassure the values of civic participation, self-reflection, equity, antidiscrimination, and due process to create classrooms that build healthy relationships and enhance and improve academic outcomes for children of color. Racial literacy seeks to do this through honest dialogue that facilitates an Archaeology of the Self, and roots teaching and learning in culturally relevant/responsive and culturally sustaining pedagogies. Making race *and* racism visible is imperative in teacher education. Race—and the way people are treated because of this social construction—plays a major role in how teachers view their students and how students experience their education. Engaging in critical conversations around race is often missing in teacher preparation programs because teacher educators are not skilled in facilitating or in comfortably participating in these discussions. Teacher educators must build their own racial literacy so that they can credibly aid the racial literacy development of their preservice students. Building the racial literacy of preservice students encourages their constructive responses to racism when they experience it in school, society, and wherever they and their future students spend much of their time when not in the classroom—on social media and in digital spaces.

21ST-CENTURY RACISM:
PRESENTING/(RE)PRESENTING RACE IN DIGITAL SPACES

In *The Souls of Black Folk*, published in 1903, W. E. B. Du Bois wrote that "the problem of the Twentieth Century is the problem of the color-line" (p. 3). Indeed, generational racism and colorism plague us still, but what Du Bois could not have imagined was how the color line would blur into digital spaces. In the 21st century, there is the unprecedented existence of cyberbullying (Vandebosch & Van Cleemput, 2008; Völlink et al., 2013); cyber-racism (Bliuc et al., 2018; Luca et al., 2020); racist algorithms programmed for websites (Noble, 2018); Neo-Nazi, anti-Black, and anti-immigrant Facebook and Instagram pages; racist tweets from a U.S. president; and citizens blasting each other with racially laden, politically charged language in online spaces. There are moments, however, that produce positive outcomes, when racial literacy intersects with digital literacies. For example, a positive outcome of the mother and toddler video that went viral on Instagram (mentioned at the beginning of this chapter) included some productive conversations among viewers of the post. Many viewers shared their disbelief, hurt, and anger, as well as empathy for the child, frustration with the mother, and other feelings, thoughts, and ideas. Some viewers who posted their reactions and thoughts did not invite a response, but others desired to engage in conversation or debate. Indeed, there were moments when viewers were speaking *to* one another trying to discern why that post happened in the first place. Constructive conversations about race and racism can and do happen in digital spaces; movements for justice and equity are born in these spaces as well.

A case in point is the 2012 murder of unarmed teen Trayvon Martin by neighborhood watchman George Zimmerman in Sanford, Florida. Trayvon's murder and the continued rash of violence against Black bodies sparked the #BlackLivesMatter movement (#BLM). Through the power of social media, what started as a hashtag quickly became an international activist movement. Cofounded by three Black, queer female community organizers, Alicia Garza, Patrisse Cullors, and Opal Tometi, the #Blacklivesmatter movement began in 2013, immediately following the acquittal of George Zimmerman. Kimberlé Crenshaw's #SayHerName campaign, a racial justice movement inspired by #BLM, started a year later in 2014 to shed light on cases of police brutality and anti-Black violence against Black women in the United States.

The rapid growth of the #BLM movement is an example of how racial literacy, expressed on digital/social media platforms (Facebook,

Twitter, Instagram, etc.), has brought about significant agitation and some change in our society. Americans who are paying attention have watched social protest movements unfold in real time via social media. In turn, we have become used to the idea of digital activism—using social media to publicize and develop political movements that expose systemic racism and racial violence. Thus, digital spaces have transformed the method by which citizens express their racial literacy, protest, and speak back to the racial and social injustices they witness in society. Activist literacies have changed the way political events, movements, and protests mobilize new supporters. For example, through episodic events, digital activism like the #BLM movement has demanded the attention and garnered the support of millions worldwide. We continue to witness through the #BLM movement a resistance to Black people's humanity being threatened and social movements in support of their right to live, to be educated, and to create sustaining forces of happiness and well-being. The #BLM movement is arguably the current generation's civil rights struggle and is a powerful display of racial literacy and a sophisticated use of digital literacy to raise awareness and bring forth change.

This book argues that at this present time in our country, citizens, and particularly citizen educators, need to acquire and build two important literacies—racial and digital—and the intersection should be taught to and developed by beginning teachers during their teacher education programs. As we approach the quarter-century mark of the 21st century, the field of education is still grappling with how to define and make sense of teaching in the digital age. The #BLM and other digital activism movements are current examples of how to use technology to teach others about oppression and mobilize millions worldwide in the fight against racial violence, injustice, and inequality.

As citizens, we are witnessing an increase in documented police brutality of Black bodies, gun violence in schools, the marginalization and cruel treatment of immigrants, and increased rates of incarceration impacting Black and Brown communities. Current research notes that there is an increase of youth involvement in online activism (Elliot & Earl, 2018). For example, @Teens Take Charge has been an active Twitter community since March 2017. The online community describes itself as a "student-led movement that's shifting the power in the education system to students!" @Teens Take Charge is an online presence that affiliates itself with Integrate NYC, a youth-led activist organization whose mission is to bring integration and equity to New York City schools. The reality is that middle-school and secondary-school–age students may well be members of these types of online and in-person organizations because they or members of their families have experienced violence or unjust treatment.

Developing racial literacy in the digital age has the potential to equip preservice teachers with skills and perspectives that allow them to grow, learn, live, and create an education system that is grounded in humanizing and technologically advanced ways of being and knowing. The development of racial literacy in the digital age can prepare preservice teachers to speak constructively against racial injustice and encourage them and their future students to reimagine a world where equity in education is possible when tied to civic engagement in digital spaces.

REFLECTION QUESTIONS FOR TEACHER EDUCATORS

Questions teacher educators engaging in racial literacy can ask their preservice students:

- What are some of your earliest memories involving race? Racism?
- How do your assumptions about race impact the way you teach your students? How do your assumptions about race impact the way you interact with others who may or may not share your racial background?
- What role does race play in your daily life? What role do you imagine it will play in your teaching?
- What do you know and understand about the history of race in America? Around the globe? In education?
- Outside of this class, how frequently do you engage in critical conversations that make space for you to talk about your experience with race and racism in the company of diverse individuals?
- What is your commitment to equity? Equality? Antiracism? Say more.
- What do you view as your responsibility to fight racism?

CHAPTER 2

How Can Racial Literacy Inform Teacher Education in the Digital Age?

> Underneath all the different interpretations of the term "critical" lies a common thread—you look at local context and meaning, just like we always have, but then you ask, why are things this way? What power, what interests, wrap this local world so tight that it feels like the natural order of things to its inhabitants?
>
> —Michael Agar (1996)

In this book, we are interested in probing the intersections of race, digital literacies, and pedagogy. We situate this inquiry within a critical framework because we understand that teaching–learning processes involving race, equity, and social change are sociocultural, sociohistorical, and sociopolitical acts. The intersection of these social constructs makes it possible to examine the relationships between pedagogical processes and the cultural, historical, institutional, and political factors that shape them. Agar's (1996) words remind us of the potential for critical theory to expose the insidious nature of racism that percolates in digital spaces in ways that can create opportunities for reflexivity and action.

Over the past 5 years, we have seen a global uptick of engagement in online spaces (i.e., social media, news, online courses, gaming, etc.) that has informed how the field of education approaches teaching and learning. More and more, teachers are expanding their learning opportunities by connecting online to extend conversations from courses and face-to-face (F2F) professional development, as well as to crowdsource and share curricular ideas (e.g., #Lemonade syllabus, #Wakanda syllabus, #DisruptTexts). Many of these educators have also made a deliberate effort to think collectively about race in digital spaces, merging theoretical orientations toward racial literacy, culturally responsive pedagogy, curriculum studies, technology, and digital literacies. As more K–12 schools become invested in digital teaching and learning—while simultaneously supporting curriculum development grounded in culturally responsive pedagogies that center issues of race—teacher education programs have to figure out ways to prepare preservice and practicing teachers to be culturally competent and racially informed in the digital age.

Each semester, we experience a growing number of practitioners who are interested in learning how to examine critical issues of race and inequity in their school, with a specific focus on how these issues manifest in sociotechnical spaces. These discussions often expose how underprepared many teachers feel to develop curricula that center the digital tools to mediate, disrupt, and reframe narratives that circulate in digital spaces, but inform F2F interactions. In 2018, a survey from the Pew Research Center reported that 95% of teens have access to mobile technology and almost all are "constantly online" (Anderson & Jiang, 2020). As we talk with our teacher education students about these data, we have yet to encounter a classroom teacher who cannot trace an in-school dispute to a comment, a "like," or a snap on a social media platform. Although we have less data about how many of these disputes are linked to racism, we know that racism (i.e., circulating racial tropes and posting racist comments) is a large part of this landscape. Therefore, we can no longer separate conversations in teacher education into two camps: one that talks only about race, and another that talks only about digital literacies. We need a paradigmatic shift that merges these conversations to understand more fully how racism undergirds the digital landscape that most students spend a majority of their time (both academic and social) navigating.

In Chapter 1, we shared the potential racial literacy has in moving individuals to action. The three tenets of racial literacy invite students and their teachers to question assumptions about race; engage in critical conversations in which they are theorizing their racial literacy development while practicing how to have constructive conversations about race and racism; and take action against acts of racism, reflect on their resistance, and spend time thinking about how these actions are increasing their racial literacy. Although we are aware that some teacher education programs are still grappling with how to incorporate culturally relevant/responsive/sustaining frameworks adequately into their required coursework, there is a pressing need to name explicitly how the social construct and actualized experience of race impacts K–12 classrooms in our current sociopolitical context. Specifically, we argue that when teacher education programs fail to make explicit how White dominant ideology undergirds the need for multicultural and culturally responsive education, the focus on race is masked (or rendered invisible) under the guise of diversity. As we consider how this legacy has rendered generations of teachers incapable of developing antiracist curricula and equity-oriented pedagogical practices that work toward social justice, we feel a fierce urgency to respond with a framework that can foster racial literacy in this digital age.

In this chapter, we review the digital literacy landscape in teacher education with a specific focus on how teacher education programs have leveraged technology to examine the impact racism has on curricula and teaching. Next, we make the case for why teacher education programs need to develop strategies for fostering racial literacy in digital spaces with their students. Then we provide examples that demonstrate the potential of using technology to explore, develop, and communicate understandings about race. To conclude, we offer suggestions and questions for educators to reflect on how they can begin to integrate these ideas into their practice.

FOSTERING DIGITAL LITERACIES IN TEACHER EDUCATION

Scholarship about digital literacies in teacher education has its origins in computing and technology. Papert (1971), a pioneer in this area, raised important questions for teacher educators to think about regarding the role of computers in the classroom. By the mid-1980s, this body of work began to promote the possibility that computers could be a powerful tool for teaching and learning and should be used in the classroom. During the late 1980s and 1990s, teacher educators were exploring ideas about computers and education that led to the creation of policy reports from the federal government. These reports emphasized the need for teacher education programs to embrace and examine the role of computers in K–12 classrooms. For example, Pope and Golub (2000) published an article outlining the following seven principles for infusing technology into language arts teacher education:

- introduce and infuse technology in context;
- focus on the importance of technology as a literacy tool;
- model English language arts learning and teaching while infusing technology;

- evaluate critically when and how to use technology in English language arts classrooms;
- provide a wide range of opportunities to use technology;
- examine and determine ways of analyzing, evaluating, and grading English language arts technology projects; and
- emphasize issues of equity and diversity.

At the dawn of the 21st century, new theories about literacy that accounted for an expansive understanding of literacy across modalities ushered in frameworks that began to account for a more participatory stance of incorporating technology into the class. In the late 1990s, researchers and educators were beginning to experiment with software on CD-ROMs like Kid Pix, Microsoft PowerPoint, and Inspiration to create content. The focus at this time was on innovation and choice, but options for creating multimodal artifacts and sharing them on the internet were limited due to software capabilities and bandwidth.

Then the National Council of Teachers of English (NCTE, 2005, 2007, 2018, 2019) published position statements, resolutions, and policy briefs that outlined principles for engaging in 21st-century literacy instruction. These documents supported the creation of language arts curricula informed by technology and literacy that foregrounded the following tenets:

- developing proficiency and fluency with digital tools;
- producing information to share with a variety of audiences;
- organizing and analyzing data from multiple sources;
- evaluating multimedia texts for multiple perspectives, accuracy of content, and reliability; and
- developing an understanding of digital citizenship.

The principles in the above policy documents advocated for teacher education programs to prepare educators to develop curricula that engaged in multiple literacy practices for a variety of audiences and purposes. However, after more than a decade of scholarship investigating technology practices in teacher education programs, researchers have found that these programs are not adequately preparing candidates to teach digitally savvy students (Koc & Bakir, 2010; Wright & Wilson, 2011).

Prior to this work, scholars who wrote together as the New London Group (1996) were urging the field to consider what could be possible in literacy teaching, learning, and research when a multiliteracies perspective and pedagogy were centered. The theory of multiliteracies pedagogy focused on the resources and tools available for design, used during the designing process as informed by ideological stances and discernable in the redesigned artifact. In practice, that shifted who could be positioned as a designer and how their identity/ies, cultural and linguistic practices, and orientation in the world are reflected in the design and redesign. Researchers like Damico and Riddle (2006), Mahiri (2006), Ranker (2006), Schultz (2002), Vasquez & Felderman (2013), and Wohlwend (2009) began to introduce us to youth literacy practices that revealed the participatory and political nature of composing across sign systems with digital tools. One issue that many of us talked about at conferences or professional development workshops during this time was the lack of access to digital tools for all students to use in the classroom and how to explore these ideas during the school day in ways that centered on equity and cultural diversity.

WHAT IS GETTING IN THE WAY OF LITERACY EDUCATION IN THE DIGITAL AGE?

Literacy teacher education programs should have a commitment to prepare teachers who can develop curricula and pedagogies that capture the evolving world of educational technology. This commitment is often fraught with dilemmas that stem from the following issues:

- few faculty who have adequate experience with technology to inform program curriculum decisions;
- uncertainty about offering a standalone technology course;
- not knowing effective ways to incorporate technology into the curricula;
- difficulty finding cooperating teachers or schools that effectively incorporate technology to place student teachers with/in for mentoring;
- difficulty finding faculty able to keep up with new EdTech products;
- inconsistent Wi-Fi connections and software glitches; and
- outdated equipment and/or the inability to purchase new technology.

At times, these issues can seem overwhelming and create a sense of apathy toward using technology. Of course, these are the same issues that K–12 educators deal with and they are not going away.

As we talk with teacher educators across the country, it becomes increasingly clear that technology is not a driving force in teacher education programs, regardless of the fact that it is the primary tool reshaping the educational landscape today (Stobaugh & Tassell, 2011). King et al. (2013) reported that "Many of the difficulties pre-service teachers experienced were related to either a lack of use of technology in elementary school classrooms, a lack of functioning equipment, or a use of technology that focused exclusively on 'skill and drill' practices—displacing the use of the computer for more generative and empowering experiences" (p. 15). Keeping the above obstacles in mind, and fully recognizing that technology has a tremendous impact on literacy acquisition and teaching (Coiro et al., 2008), literacy and learning technology faculty have offered the following recommendations:

1. Technology in education should not serve as a standalone course. Instead, methods and experiences that support teachers' conceptual and practical application of technology in the classroom should be integrated across teacher education programs (Kazu & Erten, 2014).
2. Preservice teachers and practicing teachers need frequent and embedded opportunities to learn how to use technology across content areas. Teacher education programs should not assume that because students know how to use technology in their personal life, they will be able to transfer their daily experiences into pedagogical practices or curriculum design (Keeler, 2008).
3. When incorporating technology into teacher education programs, the focus should be on problem solving, process, and leveraging the affordances of the tool to support student learning.
4. Create hands-on problem-posing experiences that help students learn to teach with technology (Koehler & Mishra, 2007; Russell et al., 2003).

As we consider the need for teacher education programs to develop curricula that can support preservice and classroom teachers' ability to curate experiences for K–12 students, we have to decide how to move forward in a way that makes this possible. A starting place for this work could be aligning the content, assignments, and field-experiences in teacher education programs with hybrid textual practices tied to media production about race and equity that generate artifacts for analysis and distribution. Given the rapidly shifting information and communication technologies (ICT) landscape, we believe that exploring the potential for digital literacies to inform racial literacy development in the digital age is an important and serious consideration for teacher education programs.

ADDRESSING RACIAL AND DIGITAL LITERACY IN TEACHER EDUCATION

In the summer of 2016, we gave a talk for the Reimagining Education Summer Institute at Teachers College, Columbia University. The focus of our talk was how to cultivate racial and digital literacy in teacher education. For the past 2 and a half years, we have closely examined the literature and sought out examples from our colleagues in teacher education programs across the country regarding their efforts in this arena. In our process of coming to understand how teacher education programs have leveraged technology to examine issues of race, we found very few examples. The exemplars include:

1. The use of digital stories to deconstruct Whiteness in an urban education program (Matias & Grosland, 2016);
2. Field-based literacy courses that explore culturally responsive pedagogy through digital tools (Price-Dennis, Fowler-Amato, & Wiebe, 2014);
3. Preparing STEM teachers to engage with technology as part of becoming culturally responsive educators (Greene-Clemons, 2016); and
4. Examining how preservice teachers can use mobile technology to probe how neighborhoods and public spaces are connected to race-based policies and issues of inequities in our society (Harshman, 2017).

Across these studies, we learned the important role technology plays in helping teacher education students reflect on the sociopolitical contexts that impact the curricula and policies available in K–12 schools; in reimagining schools and communities as places that affirm students' cultural, racial, and ethnic identities and linguistic diversity;

and in helping to identify and interrupt patterns of White supremacy and racist policies, practices, and pedagogies in service of equity-
oriented approaches to curriculum design and teaching.

As we immersed ourselves in the literature and in conversations
with colleagues, it became clear that we had identified a gap in our field
that our collective work could address. Although most of the work we
read addressed issues stemming from racism, none of the projects connected racial literacy with technology as a path for preparing current or
future teachers to develop and enact antiracist pedagogies in the digital
age. Before we outline our approach to this work, it is important for us
to debunk a few myths related to technology as it relates to race:

1. Technology is not colorblind or race-neutral. Every device,
    platform, app, or software we use in our society was created
    by human beings who brought their understanding of
    humanity and race to their work. Their epistemological
    underpinnings govern how we interact with technology.
2. Technology cannot save us from racism or the impacts of
    racism. The engineers, developers, coders, analysts, and
    marketing teams associated with our technological landscape
    are not immune to living and working in a racist society; the
    vestiges of White supremacist beliefs are viable and present
    in the work they produce. That means we interact within
    digital spaces that were explicitly or implicitly designed to
    amplify racist ideologies. Each new innovation brings ethical
    challenges that are connected to analyzing data filled with
    biased patterns, with the coding and (re)coding of racist
    ideologies in algorithms that inform machine learning,
    surveillance, and targeted attacks against marginalized groups
    who are using digital spaces to name the injustices they face
    in society.
3. Technology cannot solve all of the problems related to
    equity and racism in education. It is always dependent on
    the capacity of educators to think about how to leverage the
    device to meet the academic needs of individual students.
4. Information contained on digital platforms is not always true,
    no matter how many retweets it gets. As our society becomes
    more adept in knowledge production in digital spaces, we
    are simultaneously grappling with data manipulation, the
    proliferation of "fake news," predatory apps, and platforms
    designed to harvest and use data to mislead the public about

sociopolitical topics, and an increased presence of violent rhetoric coming from hate groups. These factors create a hotbed of tension and dissension in our society that circulates around multiple markers of identity and the intersections of those lived experiences. Thus, there is a high probability that most of what people consume and spread about race in digital spaces contains unverified or untrue information that serves to reify historic divisions existing in F2F interactions.

5. Participating in online culture does not require an understanding of structural racism. Teachers and students can consume and produce digital content without the skillset to name racist interactions. To interrupt the social and emotional stress that stems from experiencing racism in digital spaces, users have to be willing to acknowledge racism in action and have the emotional intelligence to address the situation (Daniels et al., 2019).

We believe that it is important to name these myths that circulate and inform how teacher educators and classroom teachers position and present technology to students, particularly before we begin thinking about the impact technology can have if used as a tool to foster racial literacy in teacher education.

In our experience, we have frequently attended meetings that focus on teacher education and racial equity. These spaces were hostile and often left us feeling like we were on the fringe of the conversation because most of the dialogue focused on what the teacher education faculty believed they were doing right. The meetings rarely, if ever, directly addressed the role of technology, or the racism and marginalization that BIPOC students, faculty, or field supervisors had to navigate within teacher education programs. To address this issue, we invite you to think about the intersection of these two areas: race and technology integration. Figure 2.1 presents a chart to help you consider some barriers you may encounter in your program and possible solutions.

#HASHTAG NETWORKS: RACIAL LITERACY IN THE DIGITAL AGE

Racial literacy in the digital age has the potential to equip teachers with skills and perspectives that allow them to grow, learn, live, and thrive in a society that desperately needs a teaching and learning approach grounded in humanizing and technologically advanced ways

Figure 2.1. #Racial Literacy for Activism (#RL4A) Assessment Chart

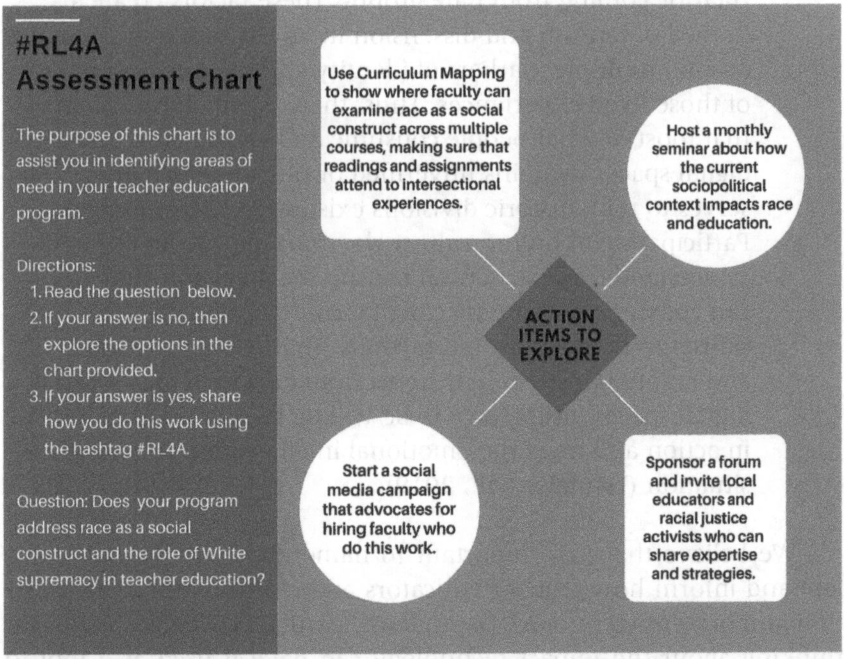

#RL4A Assessment Chart

The purpose of this chart is to assist you in identifying areas of need in your teacher education program.

Directions:
1. Read the question below.
2. If your answer is no, then explore the options in the chart provided.
3. If your answer is yes, share how you do this work using the hashtag #RL4A.

Question: Does your program address race as a social construct and the role of White supremacy in teacher education?

Use Curriculum Mapping to show where faculty can examine race as a social construct across multiple courses, making sure that readings and assignments attend to intersectional experiences.

Host a monthly seminar about how the current sociopolitical context impacts race and education.

ACTION ITEMS TO EXPLORE

Start a social media campaign that advocates for hiring faculty who do this work.

Sponsor a forum and invite local educators and racial justice activists who can share expertise and strategies.

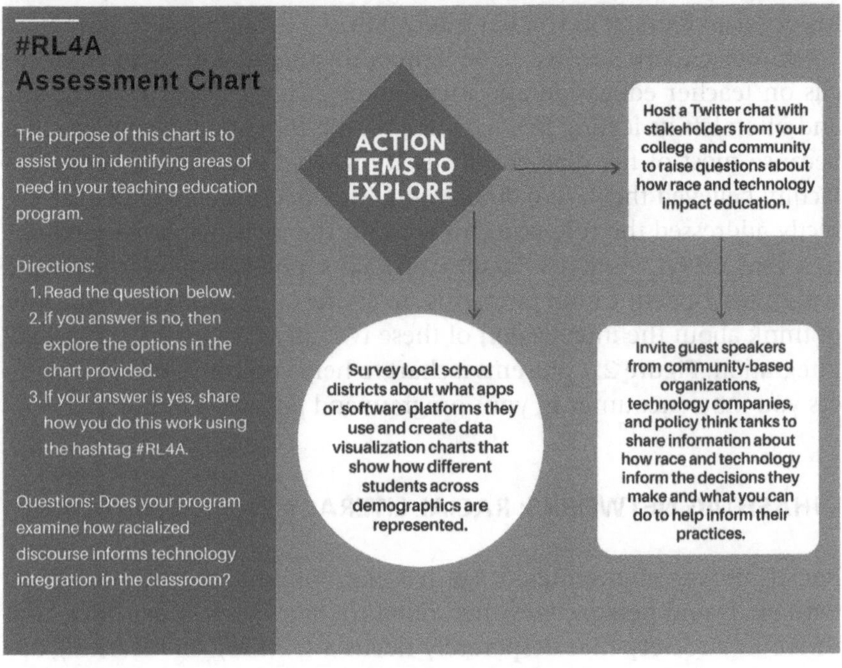

#RL4A Assessment Chart

The purpose of this chart is to assist you in identifying areas of need in your teaching education program.

Directions:
1. Read the question below.
2. If you answer is no, then explore the options in the chart provided.
3. If your answer is yes, share how you do this work using the hashtag #RL4A.

Questions: Does your program examine how racialized discourse informs technology integration in the classroom?

ACTION ITEMS TO EXPLORE

Host a Twitter chat with stakeholders from your college and community to raise questions about how race and technology impact education.

Survey local school districts about what apps or software platforms they use and create data visualization charts that show how different students across demographics are represented.

Invite guest speakers from community-based organizations, technology companies, and policy think tanks to share information about how race and technology inform the decisions they make and what you can do to help inform their practices.

of being and knowing. The development of racial literacy in the digital age can specifically help teachers speak against racial injustice and encourage their students to use tools in digital spaces that promote participatory engagement and encourage them to reimagine a world where educational equity is tied to civic engagement in digital spaces.

Figure 2.2 samples a series of social media posts and newspaper and television station reports that capture the ways race, racism, power, and education converge in the lives of students on a daily basis. As you examine each, think about how a #RL4A lens could be used to make sense of institutional structures that create space for these interactions across different educational contexts. What responsibilities do teachers have to address these issues with students?

Figure 2.2. The Racialized Ecosystem in Digital Spaces

Media/ Social Media Platform	Topic	Summary of Content
Twitter	White Nationalism	White teens from Newport Harbor High School and Costa Mesa High School in Orange County, CA, posted images of themselves making swastikas and giving Nazi salutes.
New York Daily News	Enslavement of African People	Westchester County, NY, 5th-grade teacher held a pretend auction of African people requiring White students to bid on Black students.
Instagram	Racial Violence Racial Trauma	White school principal and three White teachers posed, smiling, with a noose.
Instagram	Racial Violence Racial Trauma	Highland Park Middle School teacher is captured on video calling her students "f****** n*****s."
Binghamton Press and Sun Connect	Sexual Assault	East Middle School in Binghamton, NY, denied conducting strip search on four 12-year-old girls.
ABC7/WJLA-TV	Enslavement of African People	Students at Madison's Trust Elementary School in Virginia instructed to play "runaway slave game" in PE class.
CNN	Race-Based Hair Discrimination CROWN Act*	A Black 16-year-old wrestler from Buena Regional High School was forced to cut his dreadlocks to participate in his school's wrestling match.

* The Crown Act was created by Dove and the CROWN Coalition to create protections from discrimination based on hair texture and hair style.

Collectively, these examples represent a small fraction of the ways educators, students, parents, and media codify and circulate examples of racism and racial trauma in digital spaces to bring awareness to what is happening in hopes of igniting collective resistance and activism. This is the sociopolitical context that teachers, students, and families are navigating each day. It informs their understanding of racism, equity, and education. Students in K–12 schools encounter these racist messages and images across various social media platforms as they move between home and school communities, often receiving competing messages about how to interpret them and how to discuss relevant connections at school. Although some educators teach in ways that reflect the myth that technology is race-neutral, the experiences they and their students have in technology-mediated environments do not support this way of thinking. We argue that when educators and schools choose a "color-blind" approach to integrating technology into the classroom, they are cloaking the insidious ways that racism functions to traumatize students in these spaces. If students are using technology to conduct research, contact experts, share resources, consume media, and interact with a variety of multimodal texts, the lack of criticality of how racism is coded in these spaces can perpetuate discrimination and desensitization to racist ideology.

Every day in our society, educators, students, and families are navigating this context and becoming increasingly reliant on hashtags and viral videos to expose how systemic racism operates in our society and who is repeatedly targeted. Regardless of location, age group, social class, or other identity markers, one factor remains the same: race. Considering the potential for this context to shape education, we need to understand better what impact this racialized discourse in digital spaces is having on schools. As you reflect on this point, scan the information in the commonalities chart shown in Figure 2.3 and think about the conceptual and structural issues these examples have in common. What else would you add to this list?

Each of these examples points to systemic failure on micro and macro levels by teachers, administrators, and community members. As a society, how are we cultivating racially literate educators who are prepared to reimagine curricula, teaching, learning, and assessment and to provide students with multiple opportunities to make sense of these issues as they relate to policy, curriculum development, and pedagogy?

Figure 2.3. Commonalities Chart

We believe the journey to responding to these questions begins with an introspective look at how teacher education programs are integrating racial and digital literacies into the fabric of their programs. The type of digital literacy practices evident in the use of documentation to support an argument (a.k.a., receipts), hashtags, and posting informative threads about racism in digital spaces has transformed the method by which citizens express their racial literacy, bring awareness to social injustices they witness, and engage in cosmopolitanism as a mechanism to enact global social change. These types of "activist literacies" are transforming the way political events, movements, and protests mobilize new supporters. For example, through episodic events, digital activism like the #BLM movement has demanded attention and garnered support from millions worldwide. As we move almost 25 years into the 21st century, the field of education is trying to define and make sense of teaching in the digital age. The #BLM movement is an innovative example of leveraging technology to bring awareness to racial violence and inequality, and it has inspired educators to create curriculum that K–12 schools can use to inform students about the social movement.

BRIDGING RACIAL AND DIGITAL LITERACIES

Our commitment to exploring the potential for a racial literacy and digital literacies framework to inform teacher education is grounded in our belief in social change that is rooted in antiracism. At this time in our society, civic engagement and social change are being incubated in sociotechnical spaces. The energy that students, teachers, and activists are generating about equity and access must inform the work we do in teacher education. Our pedagogical content knowledge about race must be connected to and in conversation with discussions and debates about racism in online spaces. To advance this idea, we offer the following characteristics for a racial and digital literacies framework that we refer to as Racial Literacy for Activism (#RL4A).

The tenets of racial literacy support learners as they

- question assumptions,
- engage in critical conversations, and
- practice reflexivity.

The tenets of digital literacies support learners as they

- convey a disposition that foregrounds multimodal ways of thinking, creating, processing, and communicating ideas that go beyond technical skills;
- develop hybrid textual practices that are grounded in cultural ways of knowing;
- promote the use of digital tools to process information and demonstrate their learning across modalities;
- advocate for opportunities to make the curriculum accessible, pliable, and meaningful;
- engage in problem solving and collaboration in sociotechnical spaces to address global issues;
- express digital ways of knowing and creatively producing knowledge for multiple publics across tools and platforms; and
- identify and investigate news sources to check for authenticity and bias.

Thinking across both theoretical frameworks we wondered: How can we leverage digital tools to enhance critical consciousness about race and equity in teacher education? The six principles we offer in Figure 2.4 are a starting point for this conversation.

Figure 2.4. Principles of Racial Literacy for Activism (#RL4A)

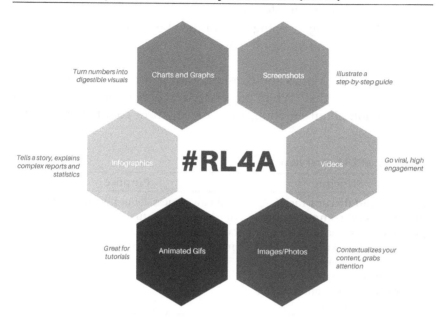

Figure 2.5 provides more information for each principle and why it matters for racial literacy in the digital age.

This conceptual model was designed to support the racial literacy development of students in teacher education programs, as well as to support their ability to develop pedagogical strategies that capture ways to embed this framework in their daily practice.

RACIAL LITERACY FOR ACTIVISM (#RL4A)

A guiding principle for teacher education programs should be to ensure that students are able to recognize, respond to, and counter racism, regardless of whether the interactions are face-to-face or in virtual spaces. To begin addressing this issue, teacher education programs will need to prepare teachers who are:

1. prepared and skilled to talk about the material, social, emotional, cognitive, economic, and political manifestations that stem from structural racism in the classroom;
2. able to move beyond their own biases to reimagine the work that is required of them to develop their racial literacy

while working to do the same through their curricula and pedagogy in schools; and

3. able to navigate doing both of the above in face-to-face contexts and in digital spaces.

For example, Matias and Grosland (2016) used digital storytelling as a medium for their White preservice teachers to engage in critical self-reflection about emotion, race, the myth of colorblindness, and

Figure 2.5. #RL4A Overview

Principle	Purpose
Identify and disrupt racist discourse and communication practices in online and F2F environments. Take note of what you observed and use these data to engage in critical and constructive conversations about the impact of racism.	Build awareness about how race is socially constructed in virtual spaces to identify racist discourse and disrupt it by engaging in anti-racist practices.
Engage in critical inquiry about the impact of racism in digital spaces.	Build awareness about the role of asking questions to: (a) trouble assumptions we have about race and racism; (b) document how we think and communicate about race and racism; and (c) make connections among race, racism, power, and equity in education that are taken up in sociotechnical spaces.
Create multimodal artifacts that trace how race, power, and equity are indexed in digital spaces.	Build awareness about the benefits of creating artifacts that use different modalities to explore race and racism across contexts.
Sustain reflexivity as a stance about race and racism in digital spaces.	Build awareness about the need to foreground reflexivity as an active anti-racist stance.
Disseminate content connecting race, equity, and activism for different audiences across modalities and contexts.	Build awareness about the role media production and dissemination can have in K–12 classrooms to foster racial literacy.
Develop emotional intelligence to address issues of bias and racial trauma in F2F or digital interactions.	Build capacity about discussing and interrupting racial bias without centering White fragility or a defensive posture.

the intellectual work required for understanding the impact of racism in education. The participants in the study composed multimodal narratives to unpack the complexities of learning about racism as teacher candidates. This genre was selected because it requires the composer to reflect on how Whiteness, equity, and power inform who they are as students and the impact these constructs have on their ability to be impactful as classroom teachers. The authors found that digital storytelling created space for the participants to name and to work to end "emotional distancing," as well as to debunk myths of colorblindness. This example exemplifies the #RL4A framework because of its emphasis on critical inquiry, creation of multimodal narratives, and reflexivity about race through the use of digital tools. The teacher education participants worked across modalities to examine race and racism and how the social construct has impacted their ability to become antiracist educators.

Another example comes from Price-Dennis's work with preservice teachers and their use of digital tools to examine issues of race and equity with culturally and linguistically diverse learners. Across her research, she has used technology as a mediating artifact for exploring issues of racism and equity within her literacy courses. The participants in her studies have created infographics using apps and platforms such as Piktochart and Canva to represent ideas about racism in education, as well as animations on platforms or apps such as Tellagami and Powtoon to teach others about concepts related to intersectionality, equity, and literacy research. The participants in Price-Dennis's study of a 5th-grade urban classroom were using technology and media to make sense of racial violence, social movements, and the impact of segregation on schools and communities. The 5th-graders and their teachers selected digital tools such as GarageBand, Glogster, and Animoto to create media that explore inequities linked to racism that they could share in digital spaces. For the kids in the study, developing content for virtual spaces offered an opportunity to share counternarratives about how policies made by city council, the Department of Education, and politicians were impacting their daily life and education. Their projects were personal and attended to the cavernous routes that racism travels in our society. These examples exemplify the #RL4A framework because of their emphasis on critical inquiry, multimodal media production, and reflexivity.

Each of these examples attends to racial literacy development across a variety of identity markers and contexts. Because racial literacy is a process and not a destination, the type of intellectual, social, and emotional work we are describing in this book has to span K–12 and higher education. Given the juncture we are at in teacher education, we believe that racial literacy is a necessary intervention in teacher preparation programs as well as K–12 classrooms. The question we grapple with is how to make sure K–12 students have opportunities to expand their racial literacy while we work with their teachers or future teachers to develop antiracist curricula informed by principles of racial literacy for K–12 students.

Teacher education programs can explore many options in pursuit of fostering racial literacy with digital tools. The focus must be on the purpose of the assignment or experience, not just on using digital tools for the sake of using digital tools, nor just on developing a skill set. Across several studies about multimodality, we learned that participants process content and generate new understandings through transmediation. Scholars such as Cope and Kalantzis (2009) defined transmediation as working across different semiotic systems to produce knowledge. Learners who have opportunities to make connections among different modalities use this process to transform one sign system into another to convey information. Considering the importance each modality holds when composing content, it is very important to foreground the affordances of each digital tool and consider how those affordances amplify the purpose of the lesson. Figure 2.6 lists several tools that have been successful in supporting students as they move from print-based literacies across different modes to compose content about race and equity in education. Each of these tools has the potential to inform racial literacy development for preservice and practicing teachers.

Each of these tools has affordances that teacher education programs can leverage to create content that promotes racial justice across digital platforms. Fostering racial literacy in sociotechnical spaces allows for spreadability of content, crowdsourcing, developing participatory communities, interacting with a global audience about topics that shape their daily experiences, and capitalizing on nuances about race and power that can be captured best through hybrid text production.

Figure 2.6. Digital Tools in Action

DIGITAL TOOLS IN ACTION

Digital Tool	Information	Literacy Practice	#RL4A
Thinglink	Interactive multimodal platform that allows you to curate and share content	Interactive Poster	
GarageBand	Create digital content about any topic and share through a variety of platforms	Podcast	
Canva	Graphic visual representations of information	Infographic	
Padlet	Online Bulletin Board	Racial Literacy Text Set	

MOVING FORWARD ONE STEP AT A TIME

Teacher education programs face the challenge of preparing teachers for increasingly technologically enhanced and culturally and linguistically diverse classrooms in a society that fails to account for the role of White supremacy in education. Research continues to inform us that teachers tend to lack the experiential knowledge to develop a digital literacies framework (Hutchison & Reinking, 2011) in their classrooms, particularly with students from marginalized populations (Price-Dennis, 2016; Seglem & Garcia, 2015). We cannot ignore this differential if we are intent on preparing teachers to take up the guiding principles of a #RL4A framework. We believe this framework can support efforts in teacher education to make visible the ways that technology is not race-neutral and attend to racial literacy development in digital spaces. Our experience working in teacher education programs helps us understand what experiences are necessary for practicing and future teachers to become critically astute consumers and producers of content about race in our digital world.

REFLECTION QUESTIONS FOR TEACHER EDUCATORS

- How are students in your program introduced to the social construct of race, racism, and racial trauma?
- In what ways do your assignments support students in exploring race, equity, and activism in digital spaces? How do you make connections between their findings and experiences students have in K–12 education?
- What issues have we not imagined yet that will matter in the next decade?
- What should teacher education programs be doing now to prepare future educators?

CHAPTER 3

Institutionalizing Racial Literacy in Teacher Education

> The paradox of education is precisely this—that as one begins to become
> conscious one begins to examine the society in which he is being educated.
>
> —James Baldwin (1963)

For teacher education programs that emphasize racial literacy development, sustained school improvement can only be achieved when there is a fundamental shift in the mindsets of educators and educational leaders regarding their Black and Brown students. It is also critical that educational policymakers shift their beliefs and perceptions about Black and Brown children and effectuate policies that are more equitable and free from racial bias to impact what these students experience in school. Certainly, while the heart of a person is involved in advancing individual racial literacy development, it is also essential that individuals intellectually understand the impact of racism and racial inequity. Engaging in a situational analysis of race allows individuals to devise a plan and take action using strategies that counter racism where they work and live. Examining how race operates as a system and affects our past and present economic, political, and social environment provides insights and knowledge to be used as resistance against persistent lies told by Whites and others about Black and Brown people and their communities. Such insight and knowledge allow BIPOC to have a deeper understanding of just how structured systems of inequality have been and continue to be. They can also identify how these systems have impacted the lives of people of color and the lives of their ancestors.

Just as racism is institutionalized within various interlocking systems, we think the idea of developing racial literacy must be institutionalized within these systems, including the education system that prepares and further develops the nation's teachers. Developing racial literacy requires educators to accept race as a major factor in inequitable systems that are present in schools (e.g., pushout policies and school-to-prison pipeline paths) and to accept how it has manifested in the education debt (Ladson-Billings, 2006) in American schools. Racial literacy in teacher education calls for self-reflection and moral, political, and cultural decisions about how teachers can be catalysts for societal change. First, it involves educators learning about systems of injustice and then explicitly teaching students what they have learned through the use of dialogue, critical texts, journaling, and digital tools, toward the end of developing their critical thinking and conversation skills around the topics of racism, discrimination, and prejudice. Second, racial literacy asks that teachers take action against injustice in their school settings once they recognize it. Finally, racial literacy requires familiarity with unconscious bias and unintentional racism (Moule, 2009), microaggressions (Sue et al., 2007), and structural racism (Kubisch, 2006). A teacher education program that fosters racial literacy must provide spaces for teachers to talk about their fears and uncertainties in embracing this type of theory and practice. Schools of education can embrace the three tenets of racial literacy development, as outlined in Chapter 1, as they move their students toward deep self-reflection, an equity mindset, and a culturally and responsive method of teaching. These three tenets of racial literacy development—(a) question assumptions, (b) engage in critical conversations, and (c) practice reflexivity—exemplify the journey of many preservice teachers we have taught over the past decade.

RACIAL LITERACY AND DIVERSE LEARNERS

Racial literacy provides a lens for viewing the effects of race on the daily lives of teachers and students. This is not meant to diminish the effects of other constructs, but to foreground the realities of living in a racialized society. As such, the purpose of this book is to build capacity for racial (and digital) literacy in teacher education by providing a framework that invites readers to rethink how curricula and pedagogy impact classroom instruction. There are myriad ways in which healthy discussion about race can stoke imaginations and possibilities in a classroom. Using texts (traditional and digital) that tackle this difficult subject in an environment where students are encouraged to look at history and reimagine a different future is required. For example, in a literacy classroom, the use of historical, fictional, and poetic texts can guide students' learning as they probe and make visible the effects of race and racism in their own education and in society.

Meeting the needs of learners who bring diverse life and learning experiences into the classroom means addressing the challenges associated with teacher preparation (Gay, 2000; Gordon, 2005; Milner, 2003; Terrill & Mark, 2000). Over several decades, teacher education scholars have developed a well-researched body of literature that informs educational institutions on how to support, advance, and enhance all facets of teacher education. The literature delineates the knowledge and skills needed for teacher education preparation, such as classroom management, curriculum development and design, and educating for an increasingly diverse classroom (Darling-Hammond & Bransford, 2005).

Notwithstanding this crucial knowledge, teacher education scholars admit they continue to struggle with the issue of race. Specifically, they note the challenges and complexity of teacher education within a pluralistic society (Asher, 2007; Ladson-Billings, 2001; Webb-Johnson & Carter, 2007) as cultural diversity in our schools increases and the American teacher workforce does not keep pace with that diversity. The large majority of the teacher workforce remains predominantly White, middle to upper class, young, monolingual, and female (Banks, 2000; Fine & Weis, 2003; Ladson-Billings, 1995; Nieto, 2000; Sleeter, 2001; Terrill & Mark, 2000; Zeichner, 1993; Zumwalt & Craig, 2008). This disconnect in teacher–student life and cultural experience has been and continues to be a concern among education scholars (Banks, 2000; Cochran-Smith, 2000; Howard, 2016; Nieto, 2000; Terrill & Mark, 2000; Zumwalt & Craig, 2008). This "cultural mismatch" often shows up as the inability of some teachers to assist and adequately support students toward their highest intellectual, emotional, and social potential (Delgado-Gaitan, 2006; Gay, 2000; Nieto, 2000). Interestingly, Sleeter (2001) suggested that even after participating in the best multicultural teacher education programs available, most teachers still feel uncomfortable, ill-equipped, or underprepared to work with the diverse school population that is currently the norm in the United States.

RACIAL LITERACY WITH A VIEW:
THE LETTER-WRITING UNIT

Racial literacy skill-building in the classroom goes beyond episodic moments in teaching and random activities learned during professional development sessions. In our teacher research, we found several noteworthy examples of what happens when teachers and students together embark on a journey toward racial literacy development. This example involves a high school English classroom consisting exclusively of boys of color where developing racial literacy was a standard practice for the teacher and her students. The students' experiences and realities lived alongside the English Common Core curriculum, and they were consistently given an opportunity to reflect on their past and present encounters with race and other social constructions affecting their lives, including their experiences in school settings (Sealey-Ruiz, 2013).

In this specific example of an East Coast alternative high school English classroom, students engaged in a unit on letter writing (personal, business, and informal). The unit was taught during the first week of a new cycle in the school year (new cycles began every 12 weeks). The teacher considered the concept of racial literacy development to be paramount for her and her students' social and academic development. Their "race letters" were but one example of how her Black and Latinx male students took up the discourse of social inequality and racism while simultaneously engaging in required literacy exercises. As the students and their teacher developed their racial literacy skills, they claimed a platform whereby they could be known—and known differently (Vasudevan, 2006)—in their school community.

In this particular assignment in the unit, students were given the following directive:

> What would you say if you had the opportunity to speak from your heart to your teachers about issues of race in school? Please start your letter with "Dear Teacher(s):"

This "Dear Teacher" assignment yielded insightful and important themes. Many of the young men said they felt invisible at times yet hypervisible at other moments in their school context. They expressed feelings of being misunderstood by their teachers over the years and shared a desire for their teachers to have higher expectations of them.

Moreover, this provocation of engaging students in self-examination around notions of race led the young men to discuss areas for which they felt they needed to be held accountable. For example, given the racist attitudes that some of the teachers had demonstrated, these young men felt they needed to remove certain behaviors that caused them to be negatively viewed and labeled. While they did not absorb blame for the unjustified racist practices leveled against them, the young men knew they had to use their bodies and voices in different ways to avoid exacerbating these attitudes. Through this particular assignment in the unit, the students tackled the assumptions they made about all of their White teachers, engaged in critical discussion, and came to moments where their reflexivity allowed them to examine their school context and their actions within the learning context.

Thus, in this classroom, students were able to discuss and critique personal experiences with race and racism as they intersected with their school experiences. They explored their racial and class identities on their own terms, and not only in relation to surrounding dominant views (Paris & Alim, 2014). In schools where students' developing identities are understood and supported, teachers can create space for racial literacy development to occur, allowing students to explore their personal histories and experiences and embrace a wide range of interests, viewpoints, and actions as an integral part of the teaching and learning process. This letter-writing unit extended beyond the classroom when the teacher and students decided the letters were important enough to share with others in the school community. The students read their letters and discussed the process of writing them with a small group of teachers during one of their faculty staff meetings. Overwhelmingly, the teachers were moved by their discussion with the students and suggested they present the letters to the entire school during one of their biweekly town hall sessions. The students, their teacher, and their mentor advisor, who was also the parent coordinator at the school, planned a town hall meeting entitled "Wait A Minute, We've Got Something to Say." Here, the young men read their letters and talked about their experiences. An excerpt from one of the letters, written by a 12th-grader, Gerald, read:

> I need you to understand that you having low expectations of me would never propel me to greatness, because no one rises to low expectations. Remember feeling sorry for us, will never allow us to grow. Meet us where we are as scholars and stop stereotyping, which continues to stagnate and contaminate.

RACIAL LITERACY TENETS AS A
CULTURALLY SUSTAINING PRACTICE

In 1989, the American Association of Colleges for Teacher Education (AACTE) released *Knowledge Base for the Beginning Teacher*. In the opening pages of this volume, school psychologist and special education scholar Maynard C. Reynolds (1989) attempted to define the knowledge that novice teachers need to bridge the gap (as perceived by education researchers) between the *art* and the *actual practice* of teaching. Reynolds presented a list of assumptions about educators who commit themselves to ongoing development in the profession. One of the assumptions read, "[K]nowledge about teaching will never be absolute or complete. . . . [T]eachers should be prepared for a career for which they are continuously involved . . . in making adaptations in their work in accord with the changing knowledge base and their own teaching situations" (p. x). While Reynolds's approach to identifying teacher "knowledge" has been critiqued for its essentializing features and the seemingly absent voices of the teachers themselves (Cochran-Smith & Lytle, 1993), we see great value in and a connection between this particular assumption about teaching and core beliefs about the racial makeup of classrooms. Furthermore, we also seek to repurpose the idea of "questioning assumptions" and apply it to the racial literacy development of teacher educators and their students in teacher education programs.

One of the first steps in racial literacy development is to question personal assumptions. Teachers must question what they believe to be true about their students (students actually need eventually to do the same about their teachers, as shown during the letter-writing unit in the high school English classroom). This is important because our assumptions often shape our beliefs, beliefs often dictate classroom rules and policies, and rules and policies codify the practices that schools engage with (e.g., zero-tolerance policies). Actively engaging in ways to question assumptions helps to uncover often deep-seated beliefs that have no basis in actual experience but are often created from sustained single stories and media-crafted narratives about students and their communities that have endured over time. These enduring scripts about students and their lives insidiously become "factual" information that teachers use to determine whether a student will experience academic and social success in the classroom. Below, we also draw on elements of culturally sustaining classroom practices as related to the three tenets of racial literacy.

THE POWER AND LIBERATION IN
QUESTIONING ASSUMPTIONS

Cochran-Smith and Lytle (1993) argued that Reynolds's assumptions list (mis)labeled a "productive teacher" as one who claims a mastery of knowledge versus being an educator who is always "standing in a different relationship to one's own knowledge, to one's students as knowers, and to knowledge generation in the field" (p. 52). Indeed, productive teachers must be prepared to reflect on their "teaching situation," which includes the children they teach as well as the multiple ways of knowing and being that their students bring to the classroom. For example, Paris (2012) noted that as culturally sustaining teachers, "[W]e understand the ways young people are enacting race, ethnicity, language, literacy, and cultural practices in both traditional *and* evolving ways. Our pedagogies must address the well-understood fact that what it means to be African American or Latina/o or Navajo is continuing to shift in the ways culture always has" (p. 91). Thus, teachers must examine their "list" that claims mastery over understanding their students' lives and lived experiences. They must open up spaces in their curricula and classrooms to examine their own assumptions and allow their students to engage in the same important work. As the proportion and volume of culturally diverse and second-language learning children in our schools increase, while the U.S. teacher workforce remains predominantly White, middle- to upper-class, young, monolingual, and female, educators and researchers must continue to identify pedagogies and practices that embrace the cultural, linguistic, racial, and ethnic diversity students bring with them to school. They must also reject the single story of what they have been told as a way to "understand" their students.

The divergence in teacher–student life and cultural experiences has been and continues to be a concern among educators and scholars of education, particularly those who study urban schools. This current generation of teachers must be able to meet the needs of students who bring diverse life and learning experiences into the classroom; they must become more effective in inviting and using the student diversities present in their classrooms. It is crucial for educators to understand and accept how students position themselves and to be tuned into the multiple identities students claim and enact. This approach creates and sustains meaningful academic and social exchanges in the classroom. As Paris (2012) noted:

The term *culturally sustaining* requires that our pedagogies be more than responsive of or relevant to the cultural experiences and practices of young people—it requires that they support young people in sustaining the cultural and linguistic competence of their communities while simultaneously offering access to dominant cultural competence. (p. 95)

Moving beyond offering curricula that are relevant or responsive to learners' lives, teachers who view their students' ways of being and knowing through the lenses of understanding and acceptance are taking a culturally sustaining (Paris, 2012; Paris & Alim, 2014) approach to teaching and learning. In our experiences as middle and high school teachers and university teacher educators, we have found racial literacy development among teachers (Bolgatz, 2005; Sealey-Ruiz, 2011; Skerrett, 2011) to be a promising approach toward creating and supporting culturally sustaining pedagogies; it has also been a viable method for developing a disposition of understanding and acceptance.

Teachers College, Columbia University, in New York City, where we have worked for a number of years as teacher educators, provides us with a great opportunity to interact with thoughtful and reflective students, many of whom embrace the social justice mission of the college. Their in-class discussions and responses in writing often reflect the work of becoming racially literate. For example, reflecting on ways she questioned her assumptions about "knowledge" that she had about others, Yuna,[1] a Korean teacher education student, reacted to a video on gender equality and representation by affirming the need to question assumptions about our accepted knowledge:

Some viewers are accustomed to accepting [messages] and lose the ability to question if those messages are right and wrong. I remember one young girl in the video said that she began going on a diet when she was in primary school. Who told her that beauty was a slim fit? The media. Why had she accepted the claim? Because no one told her it's wrong. Women are often degraded in commercials. I'm curious why no one stands up and says it's unequal. It's necessary for people to have critical thinking. I mean it's crucial for people to think about issues from a different lens and have the ability to question.

---

1. All student names are pseudonyms.

In this same class that examined diverse perspectives in educational contexts, Elasia responded to the guest lecture of a transgender Native American artivist (someone who uses their art in support of activism). In response to the lecturer's presentation, Elasia admitted that as a White woman, she always took the concept of ownership for granted. Everything in her world, from the time she was a young child, showed her that she had the right to claim her space and the possessions that were given to her. She noted:

> Ownership is something that I've always taken for granted, an essential tool for ordering our society. However, Ty's guest lecture and the thoughts of members of my discussion group have given me the space to question why I might believe that, and what structures that belief supports. My group began to pull at the link between ownership and harm, between greed and violence. To borrow a question from one of my group members, I am wondering more, "Where in my life does this view of ownership turn toxic?"

Uprooting beliefs from childhood is not an easy process. Questioning assumptions around what teachers and students have "always known" can be disorienting and creates cognitive dissonance in some individuals. However, when students are open and prepared to question their knowledge, the process can often be as liberating as it is revealing. For example, Carla used the metaphor of a treasure chest, seeing the importance of being open to examining the authenticity and validity of her assumptions. Sharing in a written reflection, she said:

> This semester—this course—invited me to open up the treasure chest and keep it open. To stop seeing beliefs as diamonds because it turns out, they never were gemstone. If anything, they were pieces of glass, reflecting my face (see: my experiences, my background, my preferences, my biases, my hopes, my fears).

Jess was much more direct about her assumptions and the need to change them. She also approached the deconstruction of her assumptions with some grace for self, recognizing the work involved in shedding the beliefs she held on to, the beliefs that gave her comfort.

> I have found that I am guilty of placing people in boxes/categories just from looking at them—on the subway, on the

street, at the supermarket—and this is people of all races, ethnicities, genders, religions, etc. What I do notice is that I am not doing it in an intentionally malicious way—I instead have the tendency, like many, to want to place people in rigid categories, I think because that feels more "comfortable," in a "this is how I was always taught to think" way. I am challenging this now. Every. Single. Day.

Indeed, it is a daily practice to face our assumptions about people and deliberately not burden them with the single stories we have about them. This becomes particularly crucial when we are talking about children in classrooms and in the communities they call home. Assumptions that have been inculcated in us as beliefs and cultural practices seem innocuous and commonplace knowledge until they are interrupted. The reflective practitioner will be able to see misalignments and contradictions once they open themselves to this type of questioning. In a final reflection of the Diversity class that semester, Eli wrote:

In my post-racial autobiography, I wrote, "For a long time, I believed that people of all colors and cultures should act and think in ways similar to myself. All people should aspire to the same goals. I would mentally praise people of color who achieved success—I did not realize that my definitions of success were restrained by my classification as a white-woman. For years, I subscribed to a "melting pot" vision of America. Now, I recognize that these ideas are simplistic and ignore cultural distinctions.

Done carefully, the work of racial literacy development in teacher education classrooms can liberate students from assumptions and lead them to the practice of taking an inquiry stance when entering classrooms—their teacher education classrooms and eventually the classrooms where they will be the teacher of record. The practice of questioning the assumptions we hold about people and places can, if exercised, become an approach to concepts and the way students approach situations. For example, Madeline had particular assumptions about what it would mean for her to be a student in a graduate teacher education course that focused on diverse perspectives in education. The format of the course—its emphasis on racial literacy development—allowed her to be open to what a class like this could be for her. This is common among graduate students who have taken (often) one "diversity" course during their undergraduate education experience. They bring assumptions from taking that course with them to all other "diversity" course experiences. Madeline reflected in class on what it meant to spend time in a course that specifically asks students to engage in the practice of questioning their assumptions. She told the class:

> Taking this course has dramatically shifted my thinking about race and racism (among other things). I entered this class thinking I knew how to be antiracist. I'm leaving it with more questions, concerns, and outrage than I've ever had, and I think that's a good thing. I'm leaving the class with a sense that I'll never be full antiracist but that I must remain engaged in a lifelong struggle to unlearn racism on a personal level and to disrupt racist structures on an interpersonal and institutional level. I've learned that the work starts by examining myself but does not end there. I'm leaving with a stronger sense of self and with a sense of purpose I didn't ever know I was lacking before this semester.

To be sure, focused and deliberate teaching around assumptions in courses that take on race, racism, class, gender, sexual orientation, and the intersectionality of these constructs is important. However, it is more important if a student comes into the classroom with an open heart and is prepared to accept that the type of culturally responsive and sustaining teaching that is needed in our classrooms, particularly in classrooms with Black and Brown students, requires the orientation of an open heart and mind. An open heart and mind not only facilitate students' ability to question deep-seated assumptions; it also positions them to engage in critical conversations that will allow them to discuss their assumptions with details involving how they came to believe certain ideas and what can shift their mindset and challenge their beliefs.

ENGAGING IN CRITICAL CONVERSATIONS

Students deserve learning experiences that allow them to be *in* conversations with their teachers about ways to co-construct classroom learning. These conversations can come about through a robust examination of the issues that directly impact their lives as well as through purposeful discourse about inequities that persist in society—including and especially in schools. Such dialogues are powerful tools that enable teachers and students to learn jointly through shared personal narratives and moments of vulnerability. Ample research has indicated that even after participating in the best multicultural preparation available to prepare educators to teach in culturally diverse settings, most teachers still feel uncomfortable or underprepared to work in these classrooms. This begs for shifting how teachers think about students and developing in them a disposition that centers a student's life and experiences as the priority—not an added value—in the teaching/learning process.

The racial grammar that permeates discourses on race and education has undergone the kind of normalization process that submerges the racialized ideologies sitting at the root of popular and mainstream discussions on schooling (Fairclough, 2014). The normalization of this language and the ideology that it represents has real consequences on the educational experiences of students. Ladson-Billings and Tate (1995) noted that Black students are rewarded for "conformity to perceived 'white norms' or sanctioned for cultural practices (e.g., dress, speech patterns, unauthorized conceptions of knowledge)" (p. 60). Further, there are indications that many Black males are treated based on how they speak or communicate with teachers and other adults in their school (Majors & Bilson, 1992).

White parents with financial means can all but guarantee that their children will go to school with other White children with financial means and learn in an environment where their child's ways of knowing and speaking will likely be mirrored by the teachers. Black parents are not given any guarantees at all. The current optics of America's teaching force also guarantees White children will have teachers—several teachers—who look like them over the course of their K–12 educational experience, thus offering White children multiple models of what it is to be a teacher and visual encouragement to consider teaching as a career. Teacher education programs continuously fail in adequately preparing their predominantly White teacher education students to properly serve children who do not share their racial background.

Teacher education programs can improve the ways they equip their predominantly White female students with a racial language to build their understanding of race in education. Based on what we know about most teacher education programs around the country

(Ladson-Billings, 2001), racial literacy in teacher education is sorely needed. A crucial approach to racial literacy development is engaging teacher education students in conversations that allow them to examine their beliefs and create new knowledge and new narratives around race for themselves and the students they will serve. Further reflecting on the whole-class discussion facilitated by the trans Native American artivist, Elasia talked about her role in gentrifying her Harlem, New York, neighborhood. She literally used the circle to make sense of what it means for her to live in Harlem with Black roommates. She shared with the entire class what she and the members of her smaller conversation group spoke about:

> We spoke about gentrification as an extension of colonization. Olive linked the ideas that Ty shared in class to the gentrification occurring in so many major cities. I shared my own guilt around this subject, and my story of moving to New York this year to live with two friends from college who lived in Harlem when I first arrived but wanted to move to Williamsburg. I didn't feel comfortable living in Harlem because of the impact my rent and my presence as a White woman would have on a community in the beginning phases of gentrification. My roommates are both Black women, and so didn't feel the same qualms about living in Harlem. Still, we moved to an area in a later stage of gentrification. I wasn't sure where to go with this line of thinking, but once we started discussing gentrification, it felt important to me to share my own position in the conversation. We began trying to parse individual and collective responsibility, bringing in Kendi's focus on the economic and capitalistic imperative of racism. Economic ambitions so quickly codified into racist attitudes and structures; that same capitalistic imperative in colonization operates on the grand scale of continents and the smaller scale of apartment buildings.

Elasia referenced one of the foundational texts of the course, Ibram X. Kendi's (2016) *Stamped from the Beginning: The Definitive History of Racist Ideology in America,* making connections between gentrification and imperialism. As a White female developing racial literacy, Elasia felt the weight of her role in the displacement of working-class and working-poor individuals from communities where some families have lived for generations. Annette, another student in the class that semester, openly shared the risks she felt in talking frankly about race and racism. She considered herself fairly conscious and aware of how inequity and inequality manifest in education. Even still, when talking about these issues with another White woman and a woman of color in her small group, she admitted, "What interested me in reaching out to Syniah and Shoshi about my opinions was the nervousness I experienced—I was worried about the judgment I would receive." Conversations that semester often went beyond race, and students critically took up issues related to gender representation and gender stereotypes. In sharing out to the entire class, Lynette said that one of her group members, Edith,

> spoke about gender-reveal parties, about how she has been to some, and had recently planned another. I don't like "gender reveals," but hesitated with how to articulate why: that the decorations and activities play off needless stereotypes; that they make a spectacle out of assigning a gender which may or may not be or end up being accurate and true; that they place so much importance on a baby's genitals and assigned sex, and seem to conflate those with how the rest of the child's life will play out.

Other students that particular semester linked the critical conversations we were having in class to taking a critical conversation approach with their students at the schools where they were student teaching. Sarabelle explained:

> It is the impact of this class. I am certain it is. I had an especially powerful moment with a student yesterday. Romeo has been very irritable in class the past two weeks—disengaged but also sharp, defiant, and antagonistic. Rather than give him a detention, I pulled him at the end of the day to talk. I led with, "What's happening? I see something different in the classroom." He immediately shared, "I'm just going through a lot of me-stuff. I'm trying to figure out who I am and it's not so easy, it's a lot." I nodded, let him share, and told him it sounded like he was doing some Archaeology of the Self work. I explained a little about our class. We decided that it's nice to share with someone after doing that kind of work, and we'll be having lunch together tomorrow. Needless to say, I'm very much looking forward to it. I already feel more like myself after spending a little time digging.

Jess spoke about the action that resulted from her engaging in critical conversations:

> I am proud to say that while uncomfortable, I have been interrupting when I hear majority problematic and harmful comments; I have been sharing videos and articles with friends and families to take our curriculum to those who could not be in a space like our class; I have been getting pushback and angry comments in return, but I have been doing it and will continue to do it because I want to engage in this work with my whole heart.

Here, Jess confirmed the heart work that is involved in bringing others along in racial literacy development work.

Sasha reflected on the importance of voice and silence in racial literacy development conversations:

> A lot of my reflection on myself and my understanding of racial literacy had to do with silence and investigating when and why it was hard for me to speak up on certain issues, especially pertaining to race and racism. Writing the pre and post racial autobiographies definitely helped me towards a deeper Archaeology of Self, to consider the ways in which I have been sheltered by my Whiteness into thinking that my voice on these issues didn't matter or wasn't needed.

Melvina recognized the power of engaging in critical conversations each week during the semester. She cultivated a habit of pushing past the level of vulnerability she often allowed herself in difficult conversations.

> I already knew before this class that I enjoyed expressing controlled vulnerability—selected stories that I tend to pull out after reaching a certain level of friendship with someone to show I'm a complicated human—but real vulnerability is exceedingly hard for me. Before this class, I NEVER in a million years would have thought I'd share something as personal as I did, but because I did, and because I survived—no, thrived, due to overwhelmingly positive feedback and support I received—I feel like I've honestly been changed. I think I'm less scared to dig

deeper now, share more openly, and maybe even cry once in a great while in front of other people.

Interestingly, KathrynAnn, another student, explored the silence that came in her relationship after having critical conversations in class and being inspired by an in-depth discussion on the complicit nature of silence during moments where speaking out on an issue can make a difference for students and others. As someone known for being outspoken on issues relating to gender equity and gender expression, she found it challenging to take up issues of race and politics in her intimate relationship with her partner. In a final reflection for the course, she thought back to a pivotal moment where her position shifted and she realized the importance of breaking silence and having these critical conversations with her partner in ways she had not previously done:

> I am rarely silent in class. In fact, I often try to force myself to speak a bit less in consideration for students whose voices are less often heard/given focus. However, in my personal life, I can sometimes struggle with speaking up. Specifically, I have thought about my relationship with my partner who is conservative. Revealing the fact often makes me feel I need to add a lot of caveats—he is not a Trump supporter, he is an avid supporter of LGBTQ rights, he is a social worker who has dedicated his life to combatting homelessness and poverty, etc. But he is still conservative and we disagree on very, very, very many points, not about values, but about policy. And I typically have not wanted to have those conversations. I have shut them down and avoided them, while he has asked for us to have them, wanting to learn about my viewpoints, and see if he can better understand the issue at hand. Our conversations about silence in the class have made me inclined to agree with my partner that breaking the silence around our political differences is important and necessary.

Oliviana, too, reflected on silence; she saw how her choice to remain silent in class during some critical conversations led her to literally silence herself *in* class, but find her voice *after* class in discussions with peers and family members on the weekends when she visited home.

The truth is I'm not sure if it was always the things that were being said in class, or if it was simply me continually fighting against my own internal barrier. There was a lot of things I didn't want to bring up in class, and that is not because I'm not comfortable talking about them, but because I just didn't find it necessary for everyone to know about these things. However, a part of me regrets not ever saying anything because it often silenced me, I couldn't always seem to get the words out. I often spent post-class talking things out with family and peers, and then sometimes even journaling trying to piece together where all of these issues and constructs, all of these expectations fit into my life, my family, my communities, and my school.

An ultimate goal of cultivating critical conversations in classrooms is for students to go beyond the audience of their peers. As with many students we have taught over the years, they understand that the work of equity and racial literacy development is not just a graduate school exercise. Rather, it is a lifestyle, a shift in their way of thinking and living their lives in relation to others. These types of critical conversations naturally foster internal conversations as well as external ones. Educators who seek to develop their racial literacy embrace the notion of reflexivity; they willingly enter the heart and headspace of examining their beliefs and values, and how those beliefs and values manifest in their actions toward others.

PRACTICING REFLEXIVITY

When teachers learn to cultivate a habit of reflexivity, it will facilitate their racial literacy development and their growth can be seen in their lessons. Gholdy Muhammad (2020), the author of *Cultivating Genius*, offers a five-layered model for equity, which is a powerful example of the types of lessons that can be created (using her model) by teachers who have deeply engaged in the process of reflexivity as they build their racial literacy development.

Teachers, like other individuals in our society, hold beliefs that are rooted in their life histories and experiences, and these beliefs are highly resistant to change. Educators who see the value of teaching in culturally responsive and culturally sustaining ways understand the need to examine their beliefs about their students and families repeatedly and work actively against those ideas and beliefs that prevent them from viewing students and families in positive ways (Sealey-Ruiz, 2011, 2013). As teachers develop their racial literacy skills, they hold up for close examination and excavation (Sealey-Ruiz, 2020) much of what they have been told and what they believe about individuals with diverse racial, ethnic, and linguistic backgrounds. Teachers who are developing racial literacy are able to discuss, in critical and edifying ways, the intersection of race, the systematic and systemic nature of racism, as well as student identities and how they manifest in schools.

Racial literacy asks that teachers identify and cultivate positive changes in their dispositions and practices. This can only come about if they are willing to be reflexive in their thinking and allow that thinking to shift their behavior positively. As it relates to the self, reflexive action is taken when someone engages in pondering life and decisions in a cyclical manner, going over actions and examining the beliefs that have influenced those actions. A goal of reflexivity is honesty with one's self and with how personal values, opinions, and experiences impact every decision that we make—and the acknowledgment that sometimes those decisions can be harmful to others. In terms of racial literacy development, a reflexive person seeks to reduce bias and shift racist and prejudicial beliefs about others that are based on stereotypes that purport to be true and accurate descriptions of groups who have been purposely marginalized.

For example, we have noticed that when many White educators begin to practice reflexivity, they often interrogate their standing in society. They engage in inquiry along these lines: Am I mediocre, or am I really as good as the world has been telling me based on my color? There are deep challenges in practicing reflexivity. One of the most obvious is entering a cycle of questioning all that one has come to "know" and understand in one's life. However, in building racial literacy toward the goal of becoming antiracist, this question, as well as others, must be asked. Individuals have to evaluate and take an honest assessment of their own abilities and be comfortable with revisiting the stories they have been told about themselves, particularly in relation to others and specifically in relation to people of color. This is most important when teaching diverse students. The first step for White teachers is to eliminate the temptation to adopt a savior complex toward their Black and Brown students. This reflexivity has the potential to expose to these educators the true reason why they are teaching and to inspire them to examine their hearts as they reach for a deeper understanding of why they are teaching and who they are within the enterprise of education. Enacting a racial literacy framework in teacher education classrooms continually instructs both the teacher and the learner. It builds reflexivity that leads to new habits of the heart and mind, and these transcend the temporal nature of class time each week or in periodic professional development sessions. The practice of reflexivity ultimately guides educators on how to best relate to their students.

Reflecting back on the conversation students were having about gentrification, and specifically Elasia's comment about moving to Harlem, Oakleigh, a student in Elasia's group, used Elasia's comments as an entry point to reflexivity in one of her written assignments.

> I was impressed by how reflective she was; moving in NYC is massively stressful, and that would only be exacerbated [by] one's status as a grad student. I think in moments of pressure or stress, it is really easy to push our values to the side in order to defend our comfort—especially as White women/people. We aren't always forced to do the work in the same way that marginalized people are. I honestly think if I could find an affordable place in Harlem or Williamsburg, I wouldn't think twice. I'm not going to beat myself up about this, but rather push myself to be more like Elasia. I see the same dedication in Joelle and SarahBeth to move this work beyond the classroom and into their personal lives. If we only practice this in front of our students, we fail to truly embody it in a way that is meaningful.

The practice of reflexivity requires a continuous return to the self—examining not only what one believes but how one acts. As poet, author, activist, and ancestor Maya Angelou often said, "When you know better, you do better." Teachers who practice reflexivity understand that their reflections must lead to action and result in a different way of being and acting. Carla, a preservice teacher, reflected on the action she needed to take in examining her beliefs:

> That's where I started this semester. It's not that my beliefs were all wrong (some were even beautiful . . . maybe not bejeweled, but beautiful), it's that I held them the wrong way. I wouldn't have said it then, but I think it's true. I held my beliefs like precious things that others only deserved to see if they would complement them. And others' beliefs? I inspected them like

a jeweler with one of these one-sided mini-monocular-things (that's the technical term, I believe) and called out, if only internally, every blemish, every dark spot I could find. . . . This course invited me to listen without planning a response. It invited me to read without pushing myself into the narrative when it wasn't about me, and without excluding myself from the narrative when I needed to take responsibility.

Preservice students who take our courses often admit some of the hardest unlearning is associated with their childhood. It is difficult dissecting happy moments that include hateful comments about others—comments spoken by those they love dearly. For example, Jina reflected on moments in childhood and how to move those moments to the action of unlearning and relearning what she had been taught was true.

Since I was a young child, I heard racist, sexist, homophobic, etc., comments which made them seem completely "normal." I was taught nursery rhymes with derogatory words scattered throughout, told I can only date someone who is White, the list goes on and sadly gets worse and worse. It is frightening how deeply our thinking can be influenced as children. In reflecting, I am able to see that what I was taught has really stuck with me, and despite being more aware and educated now, those voices are still alive in the back of my head. It will take a lot of work to unlearn what has been ingrained in me, but more powerful than the "voices" and harmful information I was fed is how much power I have to change and evolve as an individual.

In our courses, teachers are asked to confront their deeply held beliefs around race, color, and ethnicity, among other intersecting identities. They are asked to confront the lies they have been told about themselves and others; to accept what may have been given to them because of the color of their skin, and what may have been withheld from someone else for their skin color or cultural affiliation. We have frequently heard biracial and mixed-race preservice teachers express feelings of angst around race and tell deeply disturbing stories of growing up in communities that did not fully accept them as Black or White. Craig, for example, struggled with the categorizations that he felt boxed him in. He told his classmates:

I don't consider myself to be a race, a color, or a part of an ethnic group. . . . I am a man. I accept that. But I refuse to walk around daily accepting that I belong to a certain ethnic or racial group, because there are too many problems and too many commitments associated with doing so. If I say that I am White, I am a liar. If I say that I am Black, I am a liar. I am mixed race. I am two people. I am no one and everyone all at the same time.

Making racial literacy work in teacher education classrooms is a habit of the heart and mind. Educators must have engaged in their own deep work (Sealey-Ruiz, 2020) so that they can authentically invite their students to do the same. They must be educators who engage with the three tenets of racial literacy and build a culturally sustaining pedagogy through racial literacy development by acknowledging the complexity of racial identity and the permanence and reality of racism. Teachers must engage their students with this work and help guide them in becoming seekers and takers of action against the deleterious effects of racism in schools and society.

When students experience racist practices in the classroom, it only compounds the racist experiences they endure in society. To alleviate and counter these experiences and move toward healing, they must experience engagement with reminders of their humanity—their culture, language, and style of expression. Engaging students in activities and discussions that center these aspects of their identity creates space to examine and problematize racist structures in our society, and the roles individuals play in perpetuating or interrupting these structures.

For teachers of color, it is important that they engage in deep self-work to uncover and release the trauma they have experienced as students in similar educational settings. This reflection may remind them of their experiences and foster empathy and action against the ways that schools shortchange their students of color and disregard their identities and needs in the learning process. It is crucial for them to engage in this work because if they do not excavate these painful memories, if they do not dig them out and heal from them, they will likely exact harm on their Black and Brown students. They may often do this unconsciously, and view it as providing the "tough love" that children need, completely forgetting that, as children, they too craved the tender love that all children need to thrive. Teachers of color often experience the effects of internalized racism and endure school environments that are steeped in implicit bias, but they must recognize how schools are affecting them and how they work with their students of color. When this work is done consistently and properly, it is likely that teachers of color will realize that they hold deep biases toward their own people as well as toward certain others. White teachers also have these racial epiphanies, often marking the painful moments when they knew that they as well as their friends and family members were racists. They come to realize how deeply embedded racism is—even the best of us, even those who see themselves as conscious, as activists, as antiracist—because the messages surround us, because racism is in this country's water.

With determined and deep work, implicit bias can be dredged, excavated, and shifted. Antiracism is a lifetime of work because as long as our country retains the status quo of inequality, each generation will experience trauma from racism—whether from a piece of media, a conversation with a "good-intentioned" White person, or one of the myriad ways racism impacts life chances for people and is reflected in U.S. systems (e.g., health care, judicial system, education), just to name a few.

MAKING RACIAL LITERACY WORK IN TEACHER EDUCATION

A first step in a classroom where racial literacy development is at work is the fundamental understanding that racism is an ever-shifting yet ever-present structure in the lives of teachers and students. The beliefs and actions of preservice teachers must be held up for examination, and educators must guide them toward an effective change for themselves and the students they serve.

What is often left unspoken is that teacher education programs do not have robust curricula around the issue of race in the teaching and learning process. The focus remains on *cultural* divergence; therefore, conversations and change around some of the most pernicious racist acts we see play out in schools against students of color persist: zero-tolerance policies, disproportionality in suspensions and special education placements, school expulsions, a school-to-prison pipeline, and others. Creating an environment that supports and sustains student learning success is linked to the teachers' ability to narrow the gap that separates how teachers and students understand one another. As a result, the teachers' ability to make teaching and curriculum relevant and responsive to students' needs (Gay, 2000) is enhanced both within and outside of the classroom.

REFLECTION QUESTIONS FOR TEACHER EDUCATORS

- How do you engage your students in critical, reflective, assumption-breaking questions about race and other identity constructs? Think of a specific assignment, learning experience, or discussion that occurred in your classroom.
- How have you made moves to develop your own racial literacy? What is your process of questioning your assumptions, practicing reflexivity, and engaging in critical conversations outside of your classroom?
- In what ways can you reimagine your syllabus and some aspects of your curriculum to guide students in their racial literacy development journeys? What do you need to do internally before embarking on this work?

CHAPTER 4

Engaging in Critical Multimodal Curation to Foster Racial Literacy

In the poem "A Litany for Survival," Audre Lorde (1978/2020) reminds us that fear and silence function as tools that maintain oppressive conditions. Her poem embodies the sentiments many teachers share when preparing to engage in pedagogical practices that examine racism. They worry about what will happen if they say the wrong thing and offend the wrong parent, colleague, or administrator. They worry what will happen if they stray too far from the prescribed curriculum or expose their lack of knowledge about structural and embodied racist practices that impact their students' lives. Underlying each of these examples is a fear that words will fail to capture their "good intentions" or well-thought-out lessons. Either way, fear functions to maintain the status quo. Teaching and learning in contexts that are suffocating from fear-based discourse highlight the importance of Lorde's words and encourage us to push past this tension because our silence does not guarantee protection from policies, responses from colleagues and parents, or practices that evoke fear. It is also important to note the fear many educators carry and project about addressing racism through their pedagogy and curriculum does not mitigate their unrealized intentions that have a triggering impact on students, colleagues, or families who endure the trauma of racism daily. If these ideas resonate with your experience with teaching or advocating for content about racism in K–12 education, then you know how difficult it is to move past the fear and engage in antiracist practices that affirm your students' humanity by deliberately interrupting systems of oppression.

It is important to remember that injustice and racism have been built into the education system, and yet it is the education system that offers the most promising space to dismantle what Tatum (1997) talked about when she referred to the "smog" of racism that we all live

with and breathe in. Essentially, Tatum encourages all of us to cultivate our racial literacy and interrupt the cycle of racism and injustice
by constantly asking ourselves: "Am I perpetuating and reinforcing
the negative messages so pervasive in our culture, or am I asking to
challenge them?" (p. 86). Particularly for teachers, it is our job to do
that within our sphere of influence in the classroom.

In this chapter, we explore the pedagogical implications for cultivating racial literacy in the digital age. Specifically, we attend to the
role of critical multimodal curation in taking up the #RL4A framework across educational contexts. As you read this chapter, we want
you to reflect on the following questions to make visible the ways you
can implement the #RL4A framework in your program:

- What do you need to unlearn to think deeply about the
  impact racism has on your life and how it affects your
  pedagogy and ability to develop antiracist curricula?
- What do you need to unlearn to envision how digital tools
  can be used to forward racial literacy in your pedagogy and
  curriculum development?
- How can you take up critical multimodal curation as a means
  to examine the impact of racism in your teaching?

These questions are central to making sense of the content we
share in this chapter. What follows is an examination of the potential
for critical multimodal curation to function as a pedagogical strategy
and take up principles from the #RL4A framework across different
settings. We begin by providing an overview of critical multimodality
as it relates to forwarding the goals of racial literacy in digital spaces;
then we revisit the #RL4A framework through examples from different academic contexts and conclude with implications for literacy
research.

CRITICAL MULTIMODALITY AS A MEDIATOR
OF RACIAL LITERACY FOR ACTIVISM

Across our work in K–12 settings and higher education, we are interested in learning how to build on students' knowledge about the
ways race, power, and equity are coded and (re)coded in sociotechnical spaces. Specifically, we want to figure out flexible strategies for

enacting pedagogies informed by racial literacy that are loosely connected to emerging forms of participatory literacy practices taken up on digital platforms. Drawing on the work of critical and multimodal scholars (Ajayi, 2015; Freire, 2018; Jewitt, 2008; Vasudevan, 2010), we examine the potential of the #RL4A framework to function as a tool that supports innovative pedagogies in service of joy, racial equity, and justice. In this chapter, we highlight critical multimodal curation as a pedagogical strategy that can span diverse educational contexts and learners.

What Do We Mean by Critical?

We use the term *critical* to reflect an orientation to literacy practices that examines how dominant ideologies about race, language, identities, power, and knowledge production circulate in print-based and digital texts as well as in media. We position critical inquiry as a conceptual tool for educators to draw on as they work to provide a space in the curriculum for students to explore questions that are significant in their lives and address issues connected to race and equity across various digital platforms. In doing so, we acknowledge how social and historical contexts shape present-day racial discourse as well as relations, and we argue that in every place where power is differentially distributed (F2F or virtually), we need to be vigilant in locating and examining who benefits and through what means. This type of critical inquiry raises questions such as:

- What is the relationship among power and prevailing discourses about race, equity, and advocacy in digital spaces?
- Who manages the resources and power-brokering in those spaces (e.g., data, blocking accounts, trolls, bots)?
- Who benefits?
- How do we make space for these types of questions in the curriculum to support our students' understanding about how race is coded and (re)coded in digital spaces?

What Do We Mean by Multimodal?

Multimodality (Jewitt, 2008; Kress & van Leeuwen, 2001) attends to ways in which meaning is made across semiotic resources such as image, sounds, action, text, and voice. Multimodal literacy practices are tied to social and cultural ways of knowing, and they are responsive to emerging participatory practices created, distributed, processed, and remixed with digital tools. GIFs, memes, and vines are examples of multimodal literacy practices that permeate our digital interactions. These digital artifacts communicate ideas across sign systems that rely on layered representational resources to convey ideas. As Vasudevan et al. (2010) explained:

> A multimodal understanding of composing practices widens the lens of composing to include the modal affordances, identities, participation structures, and social interactions and relationships that shape and are shaped through the engagement of multiple modalities for the production of meaning. (pp. 446–447)

Applying that lens of multimodality in this book opens the door for thinking through multimodal curation as a tool for understanding racial literacy. Vasudevan et al.'s notion of multimodality maps onto our #RL4A framework because it includes constructs about identities and power dynamics among those identities as well as social interactions in F2F and digital domains, and how those social interactions influence and are influenced through the production of multimodal texts about race.

Multimodality has been written about extensively from a variety of theoretical perspectives including linguistics, anthropology, psychological approaches to literacy, discourse theory, sociocultural and cognitive theory, and critical theory. We explore the pedagogical possibilities for multimodality to inform racial literacy development across educational contexts.

What Do We Mean by Critical Multimodal Curation?

Have you ever visited a museum and found yourself in awe of an exhibit? We find it fascinating how thoughtful curation of artifacts can provide insights in so many different aspects of the human experience. Curation, or the process of selecting and organizing artifacts in a collection to communicate thematic ideas about a subject, requires the curator to be in tune with concepts, themes, and experiences across modes that will enhance the audience's experience with each artifact. Insightful curators take into account how we process information across our senses and attune their exhibits to capture the right lighting, sound effects, text, images, colors, and smells that will draw the audience and invite them to hover over certain areas. Thinking across the above ideas about *critical* and *multimodal*, we see critical multimodal curation as a process for demonstrating racial literacy in a fluid, networked 21st-century landscape. Critical multimodal curation is a process for selecting, organizing, and presenting multimodal artifacts that probe the intersection of race, equity, and power. Key to this process is the deliberate nature in which the artifacts are aligned to represent socially constructed understandings about content that provide insight into race, while shaping how the viewer interacts with content about race. This discursive practice provides opportunities for the curator to shape the content through modal choices with a full understanding that the modality is simultaneously shaping the content.

We see critical multimodal curation as a pedagogical practice that encourages learners to produce and identify multimodal artifacts to explore the relationship among power, equity, and race in sociotechnical spaces. These artifacts are later assembled to construct a narrative about racism to make transparent how themes of race, equity, and power impact our society. This practice is rooted in digital criticality and leverages semiotics to convey, interrupt, and reframe complex ideas about education, access, humanity, and equity. At the heart of critical multimodal curation is a commitment to pursue inquiry about how racism is coded and (re)coded in the discourse we use in sociotechnical spaces. When students and teachers engage in this type of inquiry, it reveals possibilities for (re)presenting ideas about race that are rooted in criticality and tied to historical, political, economic, and sociocultural literacies. Our experience with this type of pedagogy reveals tremendous potential for critical multimodal curation to examine ideological stances imbued in narratives about race circulating in digital spaces through the use of materials and tools of production that are assembled to identify, create, and/ or remix artifacts.

CRITICAL MULTIMODAL CURATION IN ACTION

What could critical multimodal curation look like across different educational settings? The following are possibilities for critical multimodal curation in K–12 and higher education classrooms. This exploration is grounded in the #RL4A framework to highlight the ways digital tools can be leveraged to foster racial literacy.

Elementary Classroom

Let us start with an example from a 5th-grade classroom in the southeastern part of the United States. Dr. Price-Dennis spent 2 and a half years conducting an ethnographic study of digital literacy practices and pedagogies in this classroom. The teacher, Ms. Jones (all names and places are pseudonyms), was committed to creating instructional strategies that highlighted the print-based and digital literacy practices of her culturally and linguistically diverse students. She worked with students in every section of her language arts and social studies classes to foster an inclusive learning environment where students think about how their strengths as learners can support collective knowledge building and advocacy for justice and equity. Students in Ms. Jones's classroom worked in multiple learning configurations throughout the day to seek answers to pressing questions they cared about in the world. They used print-based and digital tools to process and share what they learned with others. Media making in this classroom included digital six-word memoirs, podcasts, stop-motion animation films, graphic novels, magazines, and special-edition Hive Talks (5th-grade version of TEDx Talk), curated for specific audiences to advocate for gender equity, creativity, racial justice, and anti-bullying policies. All topics connected to social justice issues became the bedrock of the language arts and social studies curricula. Specifically, the students were invested in understanding why Black Americans are experiencing trauma and violence across the country.

To examine this topic, Ms. Jones shared a variety of multi-genre print and digital texts with students about activists (from the past and present) who worked collectively to investigate and call attention to the impact racism and violence have on Black Americans. The curriculum Ms. Jones and her students developed accounted for historical documentation and questions about civil rights, humanity, citizenship, schooling, protection, and disproportionate fatal encounters with law enforcement. The genres included poetry, blog posts, newspaper articles, court-case documents, maps, interviews, images, song lyrics, TEDx Talks, children's literature, podcasts, and news special reports accessed on YouTube. The students engaged with these texts as a whole group, in small groups, as partners, and individually to analyze, synthesize, and report back on important ideas that shape their understanding of the topic. The work across these configurations included curating their own magazines, creating digital infographics about police brutality and digital learning stations about Trayvon Martin, contributing questions and participating in a virtual discussion on app-based platforms about #BLM, and leading a forum about racial justice for the 5th-graders at their school. To create an audit trail (Vasquez, 2014), Ms. Jones posted tweets about their work and posted works in progress on their class website.

In this classroom, critical inquiry about social injustices took center stage as students worked to make sense of current events and topics that they heard family and community members discuss each day. To help students keep track of the emerging inquiries or important ideas they were learning about, their teacher created a class website, twitter account, and hallway display in front of their classroom. Ms. Jones had a print-based and digital audit trail for her class to make visible their questions, processes, and media making to better understand the social function of race in society. This form of curation provided insight into the instructional strategies she used to support student learning about race and equity in her classroom. Below we take a closer look at how her pedagogy supports the #RL4A framework through critical multimodal curation.

Unpacking the Framework

1. Promote critical inquiry about the impact of racism in digital spaces. Ms. Jones developed multimodal text sets for her students to support their inquiry about #BLM. Some of the text sets were shared on apps or web-based platforms such as Blendspace, Quest Bridge, Corkulous, and Flipboard, while other print-based texts, such as poems by Langston Hughes, were shared at stations or book clubs. Figure 4.1 provides more insight into the format and platform for the content.

The text sets grew in genre, modality, and complexity as the students' questions expanded. For example, students completed an online survey to provide Ms. Jones (and our planning team) information about how they made sense of the information they read and discussed in class. We met as a team to read and discuss the results and then sorted them into the following four categories:

1. the social conception of race,
2. pushing back against inequitable structures such as voting laws,
3. concerns about immigration, and
4. more context around Langston Hughes and his life.

Based on these categories, our planning team created six different digital stations for the students to complete in pairs. Each pair was equipped with their copy of the Langston Hughes poem "Let America Be America Again," writing utensils, and an iPad. Several of the activities were accessed via the classroom blog. Once the students reviewed the information online, they were required to record their thoughts on the accompanying chart paper at each station (see Figure 4.2).

Figure 4.1. Multimodal Text Set

Format of Text	App/Platform/ Participation Structure
Articles	Printed at stations around classroom
	Magazines on Flipboard
	Blendspace
	Corkulous
Photography	Blendspace
Children's Literature	Book Club
TEDx Talks	iPads
Guest Speaker	Class Forum
Social Media Platform for Questions	Quest Bridge

Figure 4.2. Reflection Questions about Trayvon Martin

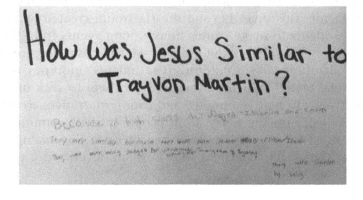

At one of the centers, students were asked to compare and contrast "Let America Be America Again" to "Running to America" (Rodríguez, 2005). Ms. Jones selected "Running to America," a poem about people desperate to seek a new life in America, to introduce another perspective of what it is like to gain entrance to and live in America from the perspective of an immigrant. Instead of creating a Venn diagram as the instructions asked, the students began to write questions on the outside of the chart template, thus shifting the focus to their emerging inquiries about race and power. The choice of how some students decided to make visible their inquiries prompted other students to respond to their questions. The following are examples of some of the questions and some responses:

> *Q1:* Why are White people so against African Americans? I
>   thought we were over this problem.
> *Response:* I agree. They're not aliens.
> *Q2:* Why are they still caring about race?
> *Response:* I don't know, but people should know.
> *Q3:* Does the author want to save America too, or is he recording
>   others' thoughts and words?
> *Response:* I think he wants to save America.

As the unit of study progressed, so did the questions, understandings, and comments students made about race and equity. This progression could be traced through their inquiries. In the beginning of the unit, students began to question the impact of race and whether it was still a problem in society. By the end of the unit, students had moved toward creating their own stations and asking each other questions about the readings, the podcasts they listened to, the TED Talks they watched, and other events where race was a salient factor. This pivot beyond the classroom created opportunities for students to make connections among events from the past and the present, such as the Trayvon Martin case, desegregation, and immigration laws. Centering the students' inquiries through multimodal texts highlighted the need for them to seek out other perspectives, alternative options, and counternarratives to the stories they heard on the news, from people in their community, or in response to conversations they had in class. For example, one student, Keith, shared insight into how he developed a question about Trayvon Martin for his peers to consider on the chart. He said: "Well, I started thinking about this photo I saw with Justin Bieber in a hoodie and thought, what if Trayvon Martin was a White boy? I asked Ms. Jones if I could find an article about this and she said yes. Then, I wrote my question." The impromptu question about the Trayvon Martin case and article selection spurred a variety of responses from the other students. Below are a few of the responses to the question: "If Trayvon was a White boy, how would Zimmerman's reaction change?"

- "I think he would have just asked him what was in the jug and bag instead of shooting him because Black boys are usually thought to be dangerous!"
- "He might not even acknowledge him."
- "If he was White he would [not] have been upset for a White person to wear a hoodie and it might not have happened."
- "He might be nice to him. Maybe [Zimmerman] would not have talked to him."

While students voiced their awareness of societal inequities and structures, their stance as learners allowed them to uncover nuances or discrepancies through comparing and contrasting knowledge sources about race across modalities in person and in virtual spaces.

2. Sustain reflexivity as a stance about race and racism in digital spaces. Ms. Jones used a variety of tools in her classroom to support students as they processed content and produced media to share their new understandings. Multimodal collaboration was part of the ecology of learning that took place in this class. An example of this can be found in how the class engaged in discussion about #BLM through the app Blendspace. Blendspace is an asynchronous platform that allows the user to view multimodal content across a variety of topics. Given the students' interest in #BLM, specifically the circumstances surrounding the deaths of Tamir Rice and Freddie Gray, Ms. Jones created a Blendspace module with articles, photography, and videos for the students to view, pose questions about, and discuss. Students could also respond to questions she embedded on the slides (see example in Figure 4.3).

Figure 4.3. Blendspace Module

3. Create multimodal artifacts that trace how race, power, and equity are indexed in digital spaces. Another example of critical modal curation from this classroom occurred during a series of critical media literacy workshops designed to complicate notions of how gender and race were represented in popular culture. Our team invited two guest speakers (graduate students who were former college athletes) to explore how racist tropes are used in media production. During the presentation and subsequent workshops, students accessed the class website and curated magazines using Flipboard (on iPads) to document, analyze, and discuss images of magazine covers and commercials. The analysis focused on how the use of moving images, texts, and pictures of women's bodies were manipulated to support a recurring trope of Black male athletes positioning women, in particular White or light-skinned women, as accessories.

During the whole-group discussion, students expressed shock and disappointment about how women were being positioned as serving men (e.g., bringing out cake for a party). In the following exchange, the students and one of the guest speakers began to raise questions about representation, media production, and race.

> *Guest Speaker:* Who do you think the ad is targeting? What do you notice about the people in the ad?
> *Student responses:* Singers/rappers/photographers, basketball players, NBA player, people who are scared to play basketball.
> *Guest Speaker:* What was most of the commercial about?
> *Male student:* Fame.

Male student: Hope. It gives people hope that maybe they can reach their dreams. The shoes just might help.

Ayesha: What about women? What were their roles in the commercial?

Kim: Doing things for people like bringing out the cake.

Male student: Partying.

Male student: Basketball is a male thing, so the glamor in the video reflects that most girls like modeling and acting . . . that's a stereotype.

This example of curating artifacts explored the ways race and gender are coded in print and digital spaces for consumption. The students and teacher made use of digital tools in the classroom to put together a collection of artifacts that helped them to trace how racist tropes are perpetuated through media and to create charts to identify strategies that can support reading against this narrative.

4. Disseminate content about equity, race, and justice as a form of public pedagogy. In the NCTE's (2019) *Definition of Literacy in a Digital Age*, the authors argued for learners to know and be able to consume, curate, and create actively across contexts to move away from consumption-only-based literacy practices. In Ms. Jones's classroom, students learned to engage with media production as a tool to amplify narratives about equity and social change. This frequently involved creating content about equity, race, and justice to make their community aware of the issue and teach others how to be advocates. For example, students in the classroom were very concerned about the increase in shootings of unarmed Black people happening in America. They were aware of the #BLM movement but not clear about what it meant. Who was involved? Why was it necessary? Ms. Jones documented the students' questions during weekly forums and daily assignments to get a sense of what they knew and what lessons could be created to support their inquiries about systemic racism, racial trauma, and racial violence.

Several units of study were planned and students worked across different learning configurations to examine this topic. There were whole-group lessons as well as small-group lessons, and students began to read children's literature and poetry about racism, racial justice, hope, and activism with partners and independently. The students created several artifacts to process the information they were learning and to share their developing understandings with the school community. They created podcasts, infographics, comic strips, poetry installations, and T-shirts. Figures 4.4, 4.5, and 4.6 show a few examples of their work in progress.

Figure 4.4. Research on #BLM

Figure 4.5. Poetry Installation About Racial Violence

Because of my skin color

There are people
Out there that will judge you
For your skin color
And tell you that
Your something that
Your not
So you have to
fight for your right

by ~~—~~

The Man Who Stood Still

"Hands up, don't shoot"
The wind blew
"Remain silent"
The rain poured
"Please don't shoot"
It hailed wildly
"Hands on the car"
Poured some more
Bang! Bang! Bang!
Thunder roared
As it poured some more
Then silence
Held with no charge
Lead to a stand
As they said,
"No More!"

Figure 4.6. #BLM Infographic

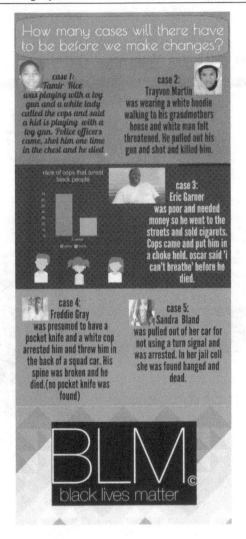

Ms. Jones provided a variety of digital platforms for students to use to learn about and create content to share about racism and racial violence in the United States. Throughout the units of study, student participation in discussions increased and new understandings about race, power, and access began to emerge. The students were excited about sharing their work outside of the classroom community (they checked the blog daily for comments) and recognized how this positioned them as public intellectuals who were contributing to the discourse on race in American society.

5. Develop emotional intelligence about racism to engage in productive discussions about the impact it has in our society. Talking about racism and White domination in American society can create feelings of uncertainty and apprehension for many educators. To cultivate learning spaces where racial literacy is used to inform these discussions, learners need emotional intelligence. Discussing the impact of racism can be an emotional experience for many learners and they need to know who they are, how to name and process their feelings, and how to be able to hear different perspectives that challenge their life experiences. Emotional intelligence begins with the Archaeology of the Self. Many learners need support in unlearning ideas they have been taught or inferred from society about race.

Educators like Ms. Jones who are committed to doing racial justice work in their classroom understand that fostering emotional intelligence is part of the labor required for antiracist teaching. In her classroom, students create charts about bias and prejudice to begin naming actions that are located in systems of oppression. Then they spend time reading about and discussing how these systems operate in books, in school, in society, and in their personal experiences. Specifically, they examine the role digital tools and platforms have in spreading mis/disinformation. The students use this information to engage in weekly discussions about their ideas, feelings, and perspectives about race, power, equity, and justice to learn how to be uncomfortable when being challenged.

Learning from The Hive Society

The students in Ms. Jones's classroom voiced their opinions about race, even when they differed from each other. The pedagogical practices and classroom environment offer a glimpse into what is possible when students are given sustained opportunities to think critically about racism and work collective solutions to address racial justice. Ultimately, the variety of digital platforms used in this classroom offer dialogic possibilities for exploring social issues. Students in the class have access to a variety of multimodal tools which, in turn, creates a fluid space for building collective responses with contrasting perspectives and sharing those with multiple audiences.

Secondary Education

Out-of-School Space: Marco Polo as a Digital "Hush Harbor" for Black High School Girls

In 2009, Yolanda founded the Racial Literacy Roundtables Series (RLRs) with three of her master's degree students at Teachers College. The Roundtables series is a forum for discussing critical issues related to urban teacher education. Facilitated by national scholars, master's degree, doctoral, and high school students, RLRs seek to cross community boundaries and promote intergroup communication, collaboration, and education. To complement the multiple perspectives that are brought to the RLR forums, the material used to initiate discussions is multimodal and includes the use of literature, writing, spoken word, social media, and video. In exploring their notions about diversity and race, RLR participants have the opportunity to learn about and from peers of diverse backgrounds and uncover some differences and common points of reference concerning teaching and learning in urban schools. The RLR Series is a space to ask questions and increase understanding of the broader community, and a space for individuals to work toward becoming more empathetic and racially literate.

1. Promote critical inquiry about the impact of racism in digital spaces. In Yolanda's work with four Black girls at a local, alternative high school, the video app Marco Polo was used to simulate a racial literacy roundtable discussion on popular and social media's characterizations of Black girls and women. Marco Polo is a free video app that mimics a visual "walkie-talkie" communication. Users are able to respond to one another in real time. The group, which naturally formed during classroom discussions, regularly used the app outside of school time, and periodically looped me in about questions and comments they had about assignments or readings, and to ask my opinion on an issue that may have occurred in school. Although Snapchat and texting were the girls' preferred methods of communication, when they wanted to *see* each other they chose the Marco Polo app to communicate. At the time of our conversations, I was also a frequent user of the app, using it several times daily to stay in contact with friends, family members, and current and former students who lived in New York City and in different parts of the United States.

2. Sustain reflexivity as a stance about race and racism in digital spaces. The group's Polo chat was inspired by an article we read in class by Dr. Carmen Kynard. Kynard (2010) discussed the power of digital spaces to serve as a modern-day "Hush Harbor" for Black women. Her article, "From Candy Girls to Cyber Sista-Cipher: Narrating Black Females' Color-Consciousness and Counterstories in and out of School," discussed the digital "Hush Harbor" her students created as a "a site where a group of black women build generative virtual spaces for counterstories that fight institutional racism. Hidden in plain view, these intentional communities have historically allowed African American participants to share and create knowledge and find their voices in hostile environments" (p. 30). Much like the physical Hush Harbor spaces of historical times, Kynard and her Black women students built and curated a virtual space—a website—to host their writing and other artifacts that were most interesting and important to them. Just as the website was for the women in Kynard's study, the Polo chat "Our Hush Harbor" was a space for the girls to discuss various ideas that impacted them. For this brief study, the girls invited me into three rounds of Polo chats within a 2-week period. All of the Polo discussions took place during out-of-school time, often in the late afternoon or early evening. The three rounds consisted of discussions around an Instagram photo of a group of Black girls on a beach, the music video "Baby Boy" by Beyonce, and the novel *The Bluest Eye* by Toni Morrison. These three topics had been brought up and fervently debated during a class discussion. Organically, "Our Hush Harbor" selected these topics because they wanted a space "free of boys" to talk more about how these images were impacting them as young Black women. Included below is an excerpt transcribed from the Marco Polo round on *The Bluest Eye*.

> *LaTasha:* Hey y'all! I had a quick question after finishing the next chapter of the book. Who protects us? Black girls are being taunted, made to feel they are not beautiful . . . who provides the defense? Maureen could have stopped the violence. She was part of the violence.
>
> *Ahkilah:* I'm not sure what you mean by who protects us, T. We protect ourselves. Black girls and women have always done that. I mean that's what the Harbor girls do right?
>
> *Yolanda:* Wait, I think LaTasha is on to something. And Ahkilah, remember that Maureen is Black, she's just light-skinned.

Ahkilah: I still don't get y'alls point.

Renee: Morrison I think LaTasha is talking directly about Black girls and boys, and how Black boys should be protecting Black girls, but instead they are beating them up. Those boys taunting the young girl. It should be inherently known that what you are doing, taunting, beating someone up is wrong.

LaTasha: Renee gets it. That's what I'm saying. It says a lot about what goes on between Black girls and boys. You know the dynamic that happens in the book and real life.

Yolanda: Yes, what do y'all think Morrison is saying there? First let me say that y'all don't need me on this chat, you are handling this just fine.

Jonette: [laughter] I don't know. I think a lot of books we read in school send subtle messages to boys on how to treat us. Look at *Native Son*. Another Black Man as aggressor. Lack of representation of black men who are empowering and sensitive. Maybe we all need protection.

LaTasha: Exactly y'all. Just like with that post and those videos. We internalize what we hear, see, and read all the time.

Ahkilah: I gotta jump off real quick. My mom is calling me. I hear you T. I'll hit y'all up later after I finish the next chapter. I might have a question. Bye Ms. Ruiz.

Yolanda: Ok Kilah.

Jonette: Look, I just feel that all of these images, all of them, give a cue to society as to who is worthy. The Black male body has been commodified from the auction block to the basketball court. Same with black women. It is widespread, insidious, and it is up to us to [stop it.].

Higher Education

#ASeatAtTheTable: Exploring Black Girls' Literacies

Another example can be found in the course #ASeatAtTheTable: Exploring Black Girls' Literacies, which we developed and co-taught as part of the Reimagining Education Summer Institute held at Teachers College. The purpose of the course was to invite educators, policymakers, and community advocates to identify paths toward developing "a more complete vision of the identity Black girls create for themselves, and the literacies and practices needed to best teach them." The course emphasizes the importance of having Black girls take the lead as negotiators of their experiences in the classroom within an educational system that has historically and in contemporary times rendered them powerless and described them as less worthy of robust educational experiences.

In the course, we explore beliefs, practices, and policies about Black girls by reviewing historical and contemporary scholarship that center their lived experiences and literacy practices. This course takes a multiple-literacies perspective to move beyond narrow print-based definitions of literacy. We designed the course to highlight how Black girl epistemologies are multidimensional, multilayered, nuanced, and complex through the use of the Black Girls' Literacies Framework (Muhammad & Haddix, 2016). The Black Girls' Literacies Framework is composed of six components that are useful and necessary for engaging Black girls in literacy pedagogies across grade levels and contexts. These components include an understanding that Black girls' literacies are:

1. Multiple
2. Tied to identities
3. Historical
4. Collaborative
5. Intellectual
6. Political/Critical

As founding members of the Black Girls' Literacies Collective, we anchored this course in the historical excellence of Black girls (which is less visible in schools and classrooms) to reduce and eliminate the disparaging statistics that do not paint a complete picture of Black girls' brilliance. Specifically, our goal in creating the course was to examine the scholarship on Black girls' literacies; become knowledgeable about the Black Girls' Literacies Framework and implications for curriculum development, pedagogy, and policy; explore teaching practices to deepen understanding about the lives and literacies of Black girls; and examine methodologies used to study Black girl literacies in and outside of the classroom.

The #RL4A framework highlights the ways our curriculum development and pedagogies serve to advance racial literacy in the course. In the section that follows, we take a closer look at our course development, pedagogical choices, and multimodal assignments.

Unpacking the Framework

1. Engage in critical inquiry about the impact of racism in digital spaces. The course began with a Facebook live talk we gave with Dr. Marcelle Haddix and Dr. Gholdy Muhammad (the other founding members of the Black Girls' Literacies Collective) that was held at Teachers College. We selected a social media platform where Black women gather to discuss issues about race, representation, and collective organizing (Carney, 2016; Sawyer, 2017) because we wanted the talk to reach an audience that is already engaging in discussions about racial equity in digital spaces, as well as to reach those who may be new to the discussion.

The purpose of the talk was to revisit the Black Girls' Literacies Framework (Muhammad & Haddix, 2016), discuss questions we were exploring through the framework, and invite the audience to think about questions related to supporting Black girls' literacy practices in K–12 education. We asked students who registered for the course and were able to attend the talk in person (or who joined online) to begin journaling about their questions and think about how those questions could shift into inquiry projects once the course launched in the summer.

2. Sustain reflexivity as a stance about race and racism in digital spaces. The course has two interactive, asynchronous modules and eight class meeting times. We launched the course with the two asynchronous modules. The focus for Module 1 (Figure 4.7) was linking the past to the present. Students were asked to watch videos, read articles, and listen to poems about political activism, collective caring, Black girlhood, and Black feminism. Students engage with each of these sources through reflection and discussion board posts and draw on those to create a visual representation that accounts for their questions and understanding of Black girls' literacies. In Module 2, we examine the "state of the union" for Black girls with a specific focus on policy and implications for teaching and learning. In this module students interact with video clips hosted on interactive platforms, read a couple of policy reports, respond to reflection questions, and play an online game modeled after Jeopardy to revisit key concepts from the modules (Figure 4.8). We deliberately chose headings that matched the discourse used to describe Black girls but created questions that challenged ideas of the achievement gap, "at-risk," and struggling.

Figure 4.7. Online Module

TEACHERS COLLEGE
COLUMBIA UNIVERSITY
A Seat at the Table
Exploring Black Girls' Literacies
PLAY

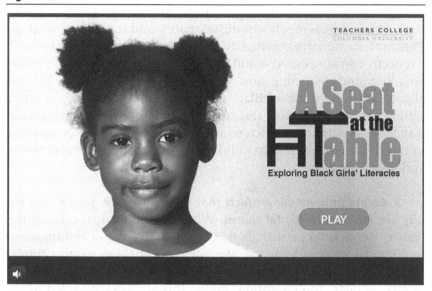

Figure 4.8. Black Girls' Literacies Jeopardy Game

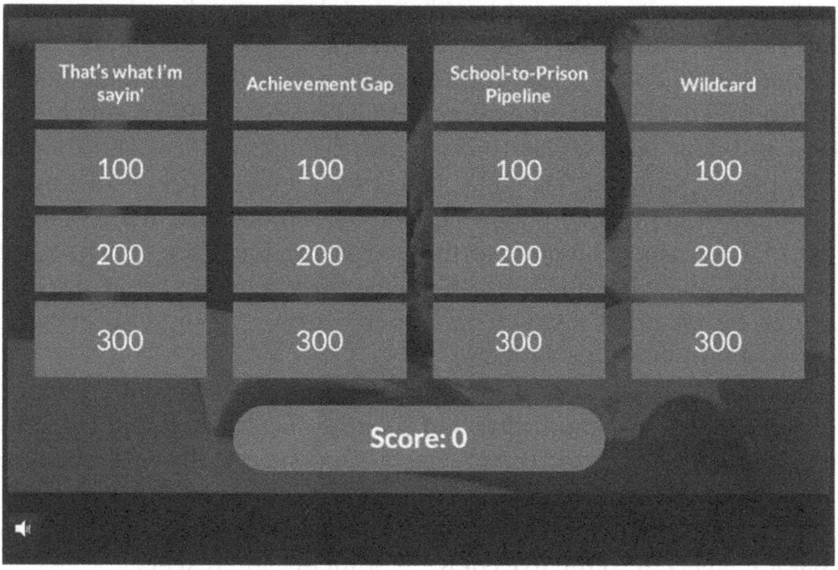

That's what I'm sayin'
Achievement Gap
School-to-Prison Pipeline
Wildcard
100
100
100
100
200
200
200
200
300
300
300
300
Score: 0

The online modules provide several opportunities for students to engage in reflexive thinking and trace the impact race and gender have on Black girls in schools, digital spaces, and community settings. This work carried over to the F2F course. We began each session with a reflective writing exercise and ended each course journaling, whiteboarding, and discussing how topics from the course and institute aligned with the needs of Black girls in K–12 education, community settings, and digital spaces (Figure 4.9). Students process their understandings in particular concrete actions they have taken or can take to interrupt and reframe harmful practices Black girls experience in various contexts.

3. Create multimodal artifacts that trace how race, power, and equity are indexed in digital spaces. When we decided to coteach this course, we were so excited about offering it as a hybrid and centering multimodal ways of knowing. We saw this course as an opportunity to center research, curriculum design, and practice at the intersection of race, gender, and education. Taking this approach afforded us the space to play with materials and topics in ways that invited students in the course to keep track of their questions and ideas through artifacts we created with print-based materials and on digital platforms. For example, students created video-based responses about race, gender, power, and education using Flipgrid; designed infographics using Canva and Piktochart to explore a topic related to Black girl literacies; and developed a playlist on Spotify to capture ideas and themes about Black girlhood related to the course (Figure 4.10). Across these multimodal literacies students curated a set of artifacts that could be used for introspection about what is working for Black girls in K–12 education and what questions should be asked and what course action should be taken so researchers and educators can support, expand, and sustain Black girls' brilliance.

Collectively these artifacts address discourse about race, gender, digital literacies, community, and identity. Each artifact documents engagement with elements of racial literacy, specifically as it relates to Black girls. These artifacts are a signpost in our journey toward understanding how Black girl is coded in K–12 education and digital spaces that are adjacent to the lives of K–12 students and teachers.

4. Disseminate content about equity, race, and justice as a form of public pedagogy. Taking on the role of a public intellectual, especially in digital spaces, can feel like a daunting task. One of the many

Figure 4.9. Whiteboard in Small-Group Discussion

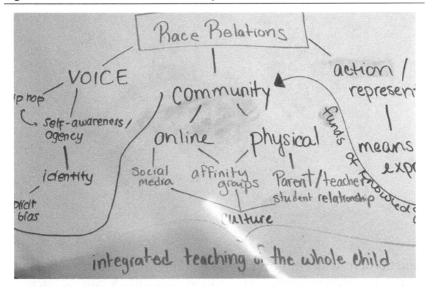

Figure 4.10. Spotify Playlist

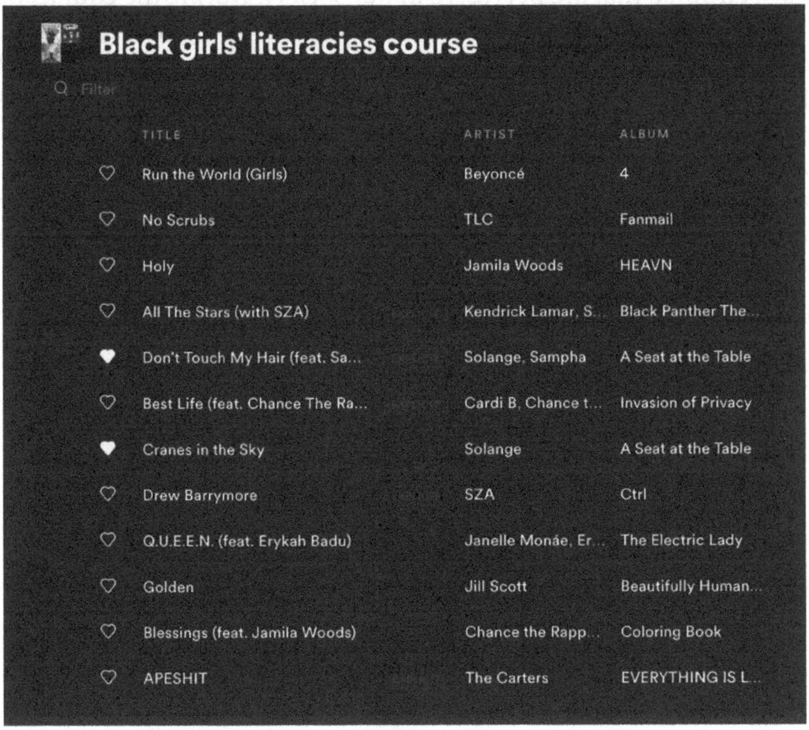

Black girls' literacies course

Q Filter

TITLE	ARTIST	ALBUM
♡ Run the World (Girls)	Beyoncé	4
♡ No Scrubs	TLC	Fanmail
♡ Holy	Jamila Woods	HEAVN
♡ All The Stars (with SZA)	Kendrick Lamar, S...	Black Panther The...
♥ Don't Touch My Hair (feat. Sa...	Solange, Sampha	A Seat at the Table
♡ Best Life (feat. Chance The Ra...	Cardi B, Chance t...	Invasion of Privacy
♥ Cranes in the Sky	Solange	A Seat at the Table
♡ Drew Barrymore	SZA	Ctrl
♡ Q.U.E.E.N. (feat. Erykah Badu)	Janelle Monáe, Er...	The Electric Lady
♡ Golden	Jill Scott	Beautifully Human...
♡ Blessings (feat. Jamila Woods)	Chance the Rapp...	Coloring Book
♡ APESHIT	The Carters	EVERYTHING IS L...

Figure 4.11. Partner Discussion: Race and Gender in Online Spaces

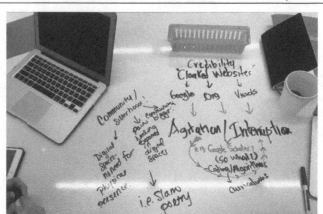

benefits of teaching this course was working with students who wanted to contribute to public conversation about Black girls' literacies to
promote impactful instruction and counter inaccurate depictions of
Black girlhood that are pervasive in our society. During the course, our
daily debriefs and assignments provided space for generative discussion and media making about race, equity, and justice that we could
share with others (see Figure 4.11). The assignments for the course
invited students to think of an audience they would like to communicate with about Black girls' literacies and then design artifacts to share
what they were learning with that audience. As such, students in the
course created ThingLinks, Tellagamis, infographics, and other print-
based and digital products to inform, inspire, and advocate for Black
girls in K–12 education (see Figure 4.12).

Figure 4.12. Tellagami

Our course was embedded in the Reimagining Education Summer Institute (RESI). Our daily schedule made space for students in the course to attend keynotes, workshops, and brown bag sessions during lunch. On the last day of RESI we shared a compilation of animations about racial literacy from the Tellagami projects with the RESI audience in the main auditorium. We also tweeted out the projects as a means to engage with a broader audience of educators who were unable to attend the institute. Our students immediately experienced the impact their public pedagogy about race had on other educators, policymakers, and administrators. They could see how others were taking notes, asking questions about the content, and Googling the platform that was used to create the multimodal artifact.

5. Develop emotional intelligence about racism to engage in productive discussions about the impact it has in our society. A question we returned to throughout the course was how do we do this work in spaces that are hostile to talking about race, equity, and justice? Specifically, how do we center multimodal tools that can produce artifacts about racism with students in these spaces to foster racial literacy? These questions represent the work that we do on a daily basis. One part of the answer to those questions requires developing the emotional intelligence of the educators in the system. If you are in a teacher education program or K–12 school and work with colleagues who cry when you name how racism functions in your setting, or immediately become defensive and lash out when you try to point out inconsistencies among the rhetoric in the syllabi, experiences in field-placements, and daily experiences of racism students encounter in your program or school, then doing this type of work is exhausting and may feel out of reach. Each of us has a responsibility to do the type of deep excavation of who we are in relation to racism in our society and to become very clear about how this relationship impacts the ways we work with or against others who are striving for an antiracist learning environment.

The course provided us with many opportunities to brainstorm ideas about how to create space for conversations about confronting racial bias and learning to sit with the discomfort those conversations can generate. We made lists of people and organizations we could consult for resources and support; shared testimonies about how we navigated colleagues who were unsupportive and hostile; named strategies we used to develop networks with people with similar interests and experiences; generated book lists we could share with K–12 students and their families; and showcased our long-term plans for continuing the work we started in the course regardless of the obstacles we know we will encounter.

NOW WHAT?

Racism is taught. White supremacy permeates everything. Whiteness, the core of White supremacy, is the tacit agreement to believe the lie that some groups of people in our society are more human than others. Racism is deeply ingrained in our psyche and society, and it will take conscious and intentional effort for teachers to become antiracist. Classroom and online spaces where racial literacy is taught and developed are among the most potent weapons educators have in dismantling the lie that binds us all. Racial literacy and, most poignantly, racial literacy in digital spaces, help teachers and students see the insidious ways racism envelops our daily lives. However, we argue that #RL4A provides a set of tools and strategies for making racist and dehumanizing discourse visible and thus available to dismantle.

When racial literacies are used to advance equity and activism in classroom and digital spaces, teachers and students are provided with an opportunity to learn and, most importantly, unlearn lessons that have led to disempowerment. Digital literacies rooted in media making that encourages racial literacy can shift the ways we talk about racism and begin to lay the groundwork for advocacy for racial justice and abolition of racist practices. It is our hope that you, as a reader of this book, will engage with the ideas we have shared with an open heart and in a spirit of radical exploration of what you can do today to make a difference. We included practical examples from our research that show the possibility of dismantling White supremacy as the rule and not the exception. We hope the content and questions we raised in this book will evoke humility and a reflective stance toward the work of antiracism that lies ahead. We end with the following question for all educators to consider.

QUESTION TO CONSIDER

- What does it mean to show up to your classroom and provide the most humanizing pedagogy you know how to offer?

Afterword

The attempted coup at the U.S. Capitol in January 2021 underscores the continued need to teach media literacy, her-/historical literacies, and racial literacy in our schools. In this timely book, Detra Price-Dennis and Yolanda Sealey-Ruiz provide a conceptual, pedagogical, and activist framework for institutionalizing racial literacies in the educational systems. They ask: How do we leverage digital tools to enhance critical consciousness about race and equity in teacher education? This question is of utmost concern to me as a literacy teacher educator—racialized as White—and part of a workforce with a greater percentage of White educators than in K–12 teaching (Haddix, 2016; Ladson-Billings, 2005). There is no doubt that the field of teacher education has colluded to uphold the status quo with regard to racial inequities. At the same time, we have created so-called progressive narratives about dismantling it. Bettina Love (2021) points out that "much of what goes by the name of 'equity work' is a collective *hoping* for racial justice. This hope too often hinges on the idea that before we change policies, we must change hearts and minds. So, equity work becomes trying to help white people learn to be less racist. . . . Under these conditions, the promise of equity is ultimately empty" (p. 1).

In this book, Price-Dennis and Sealey-Ruiz invite us to move beyond *hoping* for racial justice. They set down architecture for building antiracist teacher education. The authors stretch from research to action; historicize the ongoing crisis of racism and white supremacy; and invite literacy teacher educators to redistribute power, knowledge, and expertise leveraging digital literacy tools. The authors make the case for how racial literacy frameworks can support teachers to "navigate sociotechnical spaces with a critical lens; (b) develop strategies that support their students' ability to discuss issues of race in sociotechnical spaces; and (c) interrupt harmful narratives that circulate in digital spaces, but impact face-to-face interactions in school" (p. 6). What the authors may not have imagined when they began this book, prior to the global pandemic and schools being forced online, is the reality for millions of children, youth, and teachers around the world that school would become synonymous with digital learning. Our obligation as educators is not just to digitize current practices but redistribute knowledge and power across modalities for social justice. At the same time, students need access to print literacies, strategies for solving new words, writing powerful essays, and using evidence to design new futurities across platforms. Our students are designing digital worlds beyond what even the authors of this book may have imagined.

Dr. Sealey-Ruiz and Dr. Price-Dennis graciously invite readers into their teacher education classrooms where we see their framework of Racial Literacy for Action (#RL4A) in practice. The authors' framework for racial literacy development starts from a base of critical love and humility and then proceeds to critical reflection and building historical literacy, an archaeology of the self, and interruption. This framework provides educational leaders with a firm conceptual foundation for understanding the archaeology of racial literacy as an individual and community endeavor. The authors write, "Racial literacy can be seen as part of the 'movement' that views educational spaces as grassroots organizing sites that prepare individuals for the 'racial battles' they will fight for equity and equality in schools and society" (p. 25). The book is rich with examples of digital tools and worked examples—projects that, collectively, illustrate the constant flux and renovation of digital literacies. Likewise, institutional racism shape shifts, and thus our ability to critically read, resist, and redesign racial literacy practices is of paramount importance. The authors show us how racially conscious teacher educators may engage the racial literacy practices that were never invited into schools and use them to change the system.

Encountering my scholarship in racial literacy as I read this book caused me to pause and reflect on my journey (Rogers & Mosley, 2006). Early in the 2000s, as an assistant professor, I participated in a week-long intensive Dismantling Racism Institute for Educators facilitated by the National Conference for Community and Justice. Educational leaders from the St. Louis area—BIPOC and White—came together for racial caucus groups and multiracial workshops and activities, with self-examination following each exercise. To this day, I remember one of our facilitators telling us to "lean into the discomfort because that is where learning is occurring." It was not until I was an adult that I learned about the history and meanings of whiteness and how systemic racism is upheld by White privilege and internalized oppression.

Most White people grow up in school systems that refuse to recognize and interrupt whiteness. This dis-ease stands in the way of connecting with ancestors, reconciling and repatriating our unearned benefits from the genocide of Indigenous people and the institution of slavery, and effectively dismantling racism—a system that hurts all of us—with our BIPOC friends, family, and colleagues.

Dismantling racism and creating antiracist policies and practices is a lifelong journey that, for me, deepens with every antiracism institute I attend or facilitate, every policy committee I am a part of, every book I read and discuss, and every time I take to the streets with other parents demanding that Black Lives Matter. This is the kind of personal excavation work—done in community—that the authors call on us as a field to engage in at the *same time* we bring in antiracist frameworks to rewrite policies (from syllabi to hiring and retention policies) that will institutionalize racial justice. It is clear that it is long past time to get serious about holding each other accountable. The authors of this book join with the voices of major professional organizations that call us to do so: From CCCC's "This Ain't Another Statement! This is a DEMAND for Black Linguistic Justice!"; and LRA's statement "The Role of Literacy Research in Racism and Racial Violence"; and NCTE's "Statement Affirming #BlackLivesMatter"; and AERA's "Statement in Support of Anti-Racist Education"; and ILA's "Overcoming Racial Injustice: A Call to Action"; to ELATE's "Statement on State-Sanctioned Anti-Black Racism and Violence: A Commitment to Antiracist Instruction in English Language Arts"; and more . . .

We need to move beyond writing statements to writing antiracist policies. We need to lean into the discomfort as we further our own excavation of the self, disrupt the hegemony of whiteness, and work toward collective liberation. This book will be a precious guide along the way. The authors have invited us to share our own examples of enacting the Racial Literacy for Activism Framework using the #RL4A hashtag. Let's collectively plan to rise to their call.

—Rebecca Rogers, Curators' Distinguished Research Professor in
the College of Education, University of Missouri-St. Louis

AFTERWORD REFERENCES

American Educational Research Association.(2020). *Statement in support of antiracist education.* https://www.aera.net/Newsroom/Statement-in-Support-of-Anti-Racist-Education

Conference on College Composition and Communication. (2020). *This ain't another statement! This is a DEMAND for Black linguistic justice!* https://cccc.ncte.org/cccc/demand-for-black-linguistic-justice

Haddix, M. (2016). *Cultivating racial and linguistic diversity in literacy teacher education: Teachers like me.* Routledge.

ILA Staff. (2020, June 19). *Overcoming racial injustice: A call to action.* https://www.literacyworldwide.org/blog/literacy-now/2020/06/19/overcoming-racial-injustice-a-call-to-action

Ladson-Billings, G. (2005). Is the team all right? Diversity and teacher education. *Journal of Teacher Education, 56*(3), 229–234.

Love, B. (2021). How to make antiracism more than a performance. *Education Week.* www.edweek.org/leadership/opinion-empty-promises-of-equity/2021/01

National Council of Teacher Education. (2015). *Statement affirming #BlackLivesMatter.* https://ncte.org/wp-content/uploads/2020/04/Statement_Affirming_Black LivesMatter.pdf

National Council of Teacher Education. (2020). *ELATE statement on state-sanctioned anti-Black racism and violence: A commitment to antiracist instruction in English language arts.* https://ncte.org/groups/elate/elate-antiracist-instruction/

Rogers, R., & Mosley, M. (2006). Racial literacy in a second grade working class classroom: Critical race theory, whiteness studies, and literacy research. *Reading Research Quarterly, 41*(4), 462–495.

References

Adams, M., Bell, L. A., & Griffin, P. (2007). *Teaching for diversity and social justice* (2nd ed.). Routledge.

Agar, M. H. (1996). *The professional stranger: An informal introduction to ethnography* (vol. 2). Academic Press.

Ajayi, L. (2015). Critical multimodal literacy: How Nigerian female students critique texts and reconstruct unequal social structures. *Journal of Literacy Research, 47*(2), 216–244. https://doi.org/10.1177/1086296X15618478

Anderson, M., & Jiang, J. (2020, August 14). *Teens, social media & technology 2018.* Pew Research Center: Internet & Technology. https://www.pewresearch.org/internet/2018/05/31/teens-social-media-technology-2018/

Arunasalam, N. (2017). Reflexivity: Personal, professional, and researcher stances. *SAGE Research Methods Cases.* https://doi.org/10.4135/9781473996717

Asher, N. (2007). Made in the (multicultural) U.S.A.: Unpacking tensions of race, culture, gender, and sexuality in education. *Educational Researcher, 36*(2), 65–73. https://doi.org/10.3102/0013189X07299188

Baldwin, J. (1963, December 21). A talk to teachers. *The Saturday Review,* 42–44.

Baldwin, J. (1963). *The fire next time.* The Dial Press.

Banks, J. A. (1975). *Teaching strategies for ethnic studies.* Allyn and Bacon.

Banks, J. A. (2000). The social construction of difference and the quest for educational equity. In R. S. Brandt (Ed.), *Education for the new century* (pp. 21–45). Association for Supervision and Curriculum Development.

Barnwell, P. (2020, September). Digital divides and COVID-19: A conversation with Ernest Morrell and Yolanda Sealey-Ruiz. *The Council Chronicle (NCTE), 30*(1). https://library.ncte.org/journals/CC/issues/v30-1/30864

Bell, D. A., Jr. (1980). *Brown v. Board of Education* and the Interest-Convergence Dilemma. *Harvard Law Review, 93*(3), 518–533. http://www.jstor.org/stable/1340546

Bell, D. (1983, April). Learning from our losses: Is school desegregation still feasible in the 1980s? *Phi Delta Kappan, 64*(8), 572–575. https://www.jstor.org/stable/20386808

Bell, D. (2002). *Ethical ambition: Living a life of meaning and worth.* Bloomsbury.

Bell, D. (2004). *Silent covenants:* Brown v. Board of Education *and the unfulfilled hopes for racial reform.* Oxford University Press.

Bell, D. (with Alexander, M.). (2018). *Faces at the bottom of the well: The permanence of racism.* Basic Books. (Original work published 1992)

Bell, L. A. (2010). *Storytelling for social justice: Connecting narrative and the arts in antiracist teaching*. Routledge.

Benjamin, R. (2019). *Race after technology: Abolitionist tools for the new Jim Crow*. Polity.

Bliuc, A. M., Faulkner, N., Jakubowicz, A., & McGarty. (2018, October). Online networks of racial hate: A systematic review of 10 years of research on cyberracism. *Computers in Human Behavior, 87,* 75–86. https://doi.org/10.1016/j.chb.2018.05.026

Bolgatz, J. (2005). *Talking race in the classroom*. Teachers College Press.

Brown, K. D. (2014). Teaching in color: A critical race theory in education analysis of the literature on preservice teachers of color and teacher education in the US. *Race, Ethnicity & Education, 17*(3), 326–345. https://doi.org/10.1080/1361 3324.2013.832921

Carney, N. (2016). All lives matter, but so does race: Black Lives Matter and the evolving role of social media. *Humanity & Society, 40*(2), 180–199. https://doi.org/10.1177/0160597616643868

Carrington, S., & Selva, G. (2010, February). Critical social theory and transformative learning: Evidence in pre-service teachers' service-learning reflection logs. *Higher Education Research and Development, 29*(1), 45–57. https://doi.org/10.1080/07294360903421384

Churchill, W. (1995). White studies: The intellectual imperialism of U.S. higher education. In *Since predator came: Notes from the struggle for American Indian liberation* (pp. 245–264). AIGIS Publications.

Cochran-Smith, M. (2000). Blind vision: Unlearning racism in teacher education. *Harvard Educational Review, 70*(2), 157–190. https://doi.org/10.17763/HAER.70.2.E77X215054558564

Cochran-Smith, M., & Lytle, S. (1993). *Inside/outside: Teacher research and knowledge*. Teachers College Press.

Coiro, J., Knobel, M., Lankshear, C., & Leu, D. J. (Eds.). (2008). *Handbook of research on new literacies*. Routledge.

Cope, B., & Kalantzis, M. (2009). "Multiliteracies": New literacies, new learning. *Pedagogies: An International Journal, 4*(3), 164–195.

Crenshaw, K. (1991). Mapping the margins: Identity politics, intersectionality, and violence against women. *Stanford Law Review, 43*(6), 1241–1299. https://doi.org/10.2307/1229039

Damico, J., & Riddle, R. (2006). Exploring freedom and leaving a legacy: Enacting new literacies with digital texts in the elementary classroom. *Language Arts, 84*(1), 34–44.

Daniels, J., Nkonde, M., & Mir, D. (2019). *Advancing racial literacy in tech*. Data & Society.

Darling-Hammond, L., & Bransford, J. (2005). *Preparing teachers for a changing world: What teachers should learn and be able to do*. Jossey-Bass.

Delgado-Gaitan, C. (2006). *Building culturally responsive classrooms: A guide for K–6 teachers*. Corwin.

Du Bois, W. E. B. (1903). *The souls of black folk: Essays and sketches*. A. G. McClurg, Johnson Reprint Corp.

Elliot, T., & Earl, J. (2018). Organizing the next generation: Youth engagement with activism inside and outside of organizations. *Social Media + Society, 4(1)*. https://doi.org/10.1177/2056305117750722.

Evans-Winters, V. E., & Twyman Hoff, P. (2011). The aesthetics of white racism in pre-service teacher education: A critical race theory perspective. *Race, Ethnicity and Education, 14*(4), 461–479. https://doi.org/10.1080/13613324.2010.548376

Fairclough, N. (2014). *Language and power*. Routledge.

Fariña, C. (2016, July 14). *Letter from Chancellor Fariña on recent events*. New York City Department of Education. https://www.schools.nyc.gov/about-us/news/announcements/contentdetails/2016/07/14/letter-from-chancellor-fari%C3%B1a-on-recent-events

Fine, M., & Weis, L. (2003). *Silenced voices and extraordinary conversations: Re-imagining schools*. Teachers College Press.

Finlay, L. (2002). "Outing" the researcher: The provenance, process and practice of reflexivity. *Qualitative Health Research, 12*(4), 531–545. https://doi.org/10.1177/104973202129120052

Foster, M. (1998). *Black teachers on teaching*. The New Press.

Frankenberg, R. (1993). *White women, race matters: The social construction of Whiteness*. University of Minnesota Press.

Freire, P. (1974). *Pedagogy of the oppressed* (M. B. Ramos, Trans.). Seabury.

Freire, P. (2018). *Pedagogy of the oppressed*. Bloomsbury.

Gay, G. (2000). *Culturally responsive teaching: Theory, research and practice*. Teachers College Press.

Gordon, J. (2005). Inadvertent complicity: Colorblindness in teacher education. *Educational Studies, 38*(2), 135–153. https://doi.org/10.1207/s15326993es3802_5

Greene, S., & Abt-Perkins, D. (Eds.). (2003). *Making race visible: Literacy research for cultural understanding*. Teachers College Press.

Greene-Clemons, C. (2016). Perceptions of technology engagement on culturally responsive pre-service teachers. *Journal for Multicultural Education, 10*(3), 339–353. https://doi.org/10.1108/JME-01-2016-0006

Guerrero, L. (2008). "Pardon me, but there seems to be race in my education." [Introduction]. In L. Guerrero (Ed.), *Teaching race in the 21st century: College teachers talk about their fears, risks, and rewards* (pp. 1–14). Palgrave Macmillan.

Guinier, L. (2004). From racial liberalism to racial literacy: *Brown v. Board of Education* and the interest-divergence dilemma. *Journal of American History, 91*(1), 92–118.

Haddix, M. M. (2012). Talkin' in the company of my sistas: The counterlanguages and deliberate silences of Black female students in teacher education. *Linguistics and Education, 23*(2), 169–181. https://doi.org/10.1016/j.linged.2012.01.003

Haddix, M., & Price-Dennis, D. (2013). Urban fiction and multicultural literature as transformative tools for preparing English teachers for diverse classrooms. *English Education, 45*(3), 247–283. www.jstor.org/stable/23364869

Hall, S. (1997). *Race, the floating signifier*. Media Education Foundation. https://www.mediaed.org/transcripts/Stuart-Hall-Race-the-Floating-Signifier -Transcript.pdf

Harshman, J. (2017). Rethinking place, boundaries, and local history in social studies teacher education. *Social Studies Research and Practice, 12*(3), 341–353. https://doi.org/10.1108/SSRP-08-2017-0050

Hollingsworth, S. (1989). Prior beliefs and cognitive change in learning to teach. *American Educational Research Journal, 26*(2), 160–189. https://doi. org/10.3102/00028312026002160

Howard, G. (2016). *We can't teach what we don't know: White teachers, multiracial schools* (3rd ed.). Teachers College Press.

Hucks, D. (2014). *New visions of collective achievement: The cross-generational schooling experiences of African American males*. Sense Publishers.

Hutchison, A., & Reinking, D. (2011). Teachers' perceptions of integrating information and communication technologies into literacy instruction: A national survey in the United States. *Reading Research Quarterly, 46*(4), 312–333. https://doi.org/10.1002/RRQ.002

Isaksen, J. L. (2008). Rhetorics of race: Mapping White narratives. In L. Guerrero (Ed.), *Teaching race in the 21st century: College teachers talk about their fears, risks, and rewards* (pp. 97–110). Palgrave Macmillan.

Jewitt, C. (2008). Multimodality and literacy in school classrooms. *Review of Research in Education, 32*(1), 241–267. https://doi.org/10.3102/0091732X07310586

Johnson, M. T. (2009). *Race(ing) around in rhetoric and composition circles: Racial literacy as the way out* [Unpublished doctoral dissertation]. The University of North Carolina at Greensboro.

Kazu, I. Y., & Erten, P. (2014). Teachers' technological pedagogical content knowledge self-efficacies. *Journal of Education and Training Studies, 2*(2), 126–144.

Keeler, C. (2008). When curriculum and technology meet: Technology integration in methods courses. *Journal of Computing in Teacher Education, 25*(1), 23–30. https://doi.org/10.1080/10402454.2008.10784605

Kendi, I. X. (2016). *Stamped from the beginning: The definitive history of racist ideas in America*. Nation Books.

Kendi, I. X. (2020, April 6). What the racial data show: The pandemic seems to be hitting people of color the hardest. *The Atlantic*.https://www.theatlantic.com/ideas/archive/2020/04/coronavirus-exposing-our-racial-divides/609526/

Kim, R. Y. (2008). Teaching race at anti-Berkeley and beyond. In L. Guerrero (Ed.), *Teaching race in the 21st century: College teachers talk about their fears, risks, and rewards* (pp. 71–82). Palgrave Macmillan.

King, J. R., Scheider, J. J., Kozdras, D., Minick, V., Welsh, J., Brindley, R., Feger, M. V. F., & Kirby, A. (2013). The multiple ways technology supports pre-service teacher education: A foray into multimedia literacies. *Journal of Reading Education, 38*(3), 14–20. https://scholarcommons.usf.edu/tal_facpub/6

King, L. J. (2016). Teaching black history as a racial literacy project, *Race Ethnicity and Education, 19*(6), 1303–1318. https://doi.org/10.1080/13613324.2016.1150822

King, M. L., Jr. (1966). *MLK: A riot is the language of the unheard.* 60 Minutes Overtime. https://www.cbsnews.com/news/mlk-a-riot-is-the-language-of-the-unheard/

Koc, M., & Bakir, N. (2010). A needs assessment survey to investigate pre-service teachers' knowledge, experiences and perceptions about preparation to using educational technologies. *Turkish Online Journal of Educational Technology, 9*(1), 13–22.

Koehler, M., & Mishra, P. (2007). What is technological pedagogical content knowledge (TPACK)? *Contemporary Issues in Technology and Teacher Education, 9*(1), 60–70. https://citejournal.org/volume-9/issue-1-09/general/what-is-technological-pedagogicalcontent-knowledge

Kress, G., & Van Leeuwen, T. (2001). *Multimodal discourse: The modes and media of contemporary communication.* Cappelen.

Kubisch, A. C. (2006). Why structural racism? Why a structural racism caucus? *Poverty and Race, 15*(6).

Kynard, C. (2010) From candy girls to cyber sista-cipher: Narrating Black females' color-consciousness and counterstories in *and* out of school. *Harvard Educational Review 80*(1), 30–53. https://doi.org/10.17763/haer.80.1.4611255014427701

Ladson-Billings, G. (1995). Culturally relevant teaching. *Theory Into Practice, 34*(3), 159–165.

Ladson-Billings, G. (2001). *Crossing over to Canaan: The journey of new teachers in diverse classrooms.* Jossey-Bass.

Ladson-Billings, G. (2006, October). From the achievement gap to the education debt: Understanding achievement. *Educational Researcher, 35*(7). https://doi.org/10.3102%2F0013189X035007003

Ladson-Billings, G., & Tate, W. (1995). Toward a critical race theory of education. *Teachers College Record, 97*(1), 47–68.

Lankshear, C., & Knobel, M. (Eds.). (2008). *Digital literacies: Concepts, policies and practices* (Vol. 30). Peter Lang.

Lorde, A. (1978). A litany for survival. In R. Gay (Ed.), *The selected works of Audre Lorde* (pp. 283–284). W. W. Norton & Company.

Luca, M., Stern, S., Cook, D., & Kim, H. (2020). *Racial discrimination on Airbnb: The role of platform design.* Harvard Business Publishing Education. https://hbsp.harvard.edu/product/920051-PDF-ENG

Lyiscott, J. (2017, May 18). *If you think you're giving students of color a voice, get over yourself.* Heinemann Publishing. https://medium.com/@heinemann/if-you-think-youre-giving-students-of-color-a-voice-get-over-yourself-cc8a4a684f16

Mahiri, J. (2006). Digital DJ-ing: Rhythms of learning in an urban school. *Language Arts, 84*(1), 55–62.

Mahiri, J. (2017). *Deconstructing race: Multicultural education beyond the color-bind.* Teachers College Press.

Majors, R., & Bilson, J. M. (1992). *Cool pose: The dilemmas of Black manhood in America.* Lexington Books.

Mangino, R. (2008). Teaching the "ism" in racism, or how to transform student resistance. In L. Guerrero (Ed.), *Teaching race in the 21st century: College teachers talk about their fears, risks, and rewards* (pp. 35–48). Palgrave Macmillan.

Martínez, R. A. (2017). 'Are you gonna show this to white people?': Chicana/o and Latina/o students' counter-narratives on race, place, and representation. *Race Ethnicity and Education, 20*(1), 101–116. https://doi.org/10.1080/136133 24.2015.1121219

Matias, C. E., & Grosland, T. J. (2016). Digital storytelling as racial justice: Digital hopes for deconstructing whiteness in teacher education. *Journal of Teacher Education, 67*(2), 152–164. https://doi.org/10.1177/0022487115624493

Michael, A. (2014). *Raising race questions.* Teachers College Press.

Milner, H. R. (2003). Teacher reflection and race in cultural contexts: History, meanings, and methods in teaching. *Theory Into Practice, 42*(3), 173–180. https://doi.org/10.1207/s15430421tip4203_2

Milner, H. R. (2006). Preservice teachers' learning about cultural and racial diversity: Implications for urban education. *Urban Education, 41*(4), 343–375. https://doi.org/10.1177/0042085906289709

Milner, H. R. (2010). *Start where you are, but don't stay there: Understanding diversity, opportunity gaps, and teaching in today's classrooms.* Harvard Education Press.

Morrison, T. (1992). *Playing in the dark: Whiteness and the literary imagination.* First Vintage.

Moule, J. (2009). Understanding unconscious bias and unintentional racism. *Phi Delta Kappan, 90*(5), 320–326. https://doi.org/10.1177/003172170909000504

Moyers, B. (Producer). (2016, July 8). *Khalil Gibran Muhammad on our crisis of racial justice* [Podcast transcript]. Retrieved August 1, 2019 from https://billmoyers.com/content/full-transcript-khalil-gibran-muhammad-crisis-racial-justice/

Muhammad, G. (2020). *Cultivating genius: An equity framework for culturally and historically responsive literacy.* Scholastic.

Muhammad, G. E., & Haddix, M. (2016). Centering Black girls' literacies: A review of literature on the multiple ways of knowing of Black girls. *English Education, 48*(4), 299–336. https://www/jstor.org/stable/26492572

National Center for Education Statistics. (2013). *The condition of education 2013.* https://nces.ed.gov/pubsearch/pubsinfo.asp?pubid=2013037

National Center for Education Statistics. (2018). *The condition of education 2018.* https://nces.ed.gov/pubsearch/pubsinfo.asp?pubid=2018144

National Council of Teachers of English (NCTE). (2005, November 17). *Multimodal literacies* [Position statement]. https://ncte.org/statement/multimodalliteracies

National Council of Teachers of English (NCTE). (2007). *21st century literacies: A policy research brief.* https://ncte.org/statement/21st-century-literacies-a-policy-research-brief/

National Council of Teachers of English (NCTE). (2018). *Beliefs for integrating technology into the English language arts classroom* [Position statement]. https://ncte.org/statement/beliefs-technology-preparation-english-teachers

National Council of Teachers of English (NCTE). (2019). *Definition of literacy in the digital age* [Position statement]. https://ncte.org/statement/nctes-definition-literacy-digital-age

New London Group. (1996). A pedagogy of multiliteracies: Designing social futures. *Harvard Educational Review, 66*(1), 60–93.

Nieto, S. (2000). *Affirming diversity: The sociopolitical context of multicultural education* (3rd ed.). Longman.

Noble, S. U. (2018). *Algorithms of oppression.* New York University Press.

Omi, M., & Winant, H. (1986). *Racial formation in the United States: From the 1960s to the 1980s.* Routledge.

Orfield, G. (1988). School desegregation in the 1980s. *Equity and Choice, 4*(February), 25–28.

Papert, S. (1971). *Teaching children to be mathematicians vs. teaching about mathematics.* Artificial Intelligence Memo No. 249. Massachusetts Institute of Technology Artificial Intelligence Lab.

Paris, D. (2012). Culturally sustaining pedagogy: A needed change in stance, terminology, and practice. *Educational Researcher, 41*(3), 93–97. https://doi.org/10.3102/0013189X12441244

Paris, D., & Alim, S. (2014). What are we seeking to sustain through culturally sustaining pedagogy? A loving critique forward. *Harvard Educational Review, 84*(1), 85–100. https://doi.org/10.17763/haer.84.1.982l873k2ht16m77

Pope, C. A., & Golub, J. N. (2000). Preparing tomorrow's English language arts teachers today: Principles and practices for infusing technology. *Contemporary Issues in Technology and Teacher Education, 1*(1), 89–97. https://citejournal.org/volume-1/issue-1-00/english-language-arts/preparing-tomorrows-english-language-artsteachers-today-principles-and-practices-for-infusingtechnology/

Price-Dennis, D. (2016). Developing curriculum to support Black girls' literacies in digital spaces. *English Education, 48*(4), 337–361.

Price-Dennis, D., Fowler-Amato, M., & Wiebe, M. (2014). Developing an authentic writing curriculum: Pre-service teachers explore the use of writer's notebooks and digital texts. *Journal of Writing Teacher Education, 3*(2), 46–77.

Price-Dennis, D., & Souto-Manning, M. (2011). (Re)Framing diverse preservice classrooms as spaces for culturally relevant teaching. *Journal of Negro Education, 80*(3), 223–238. https://www.jstor.org/stable/41341130

Prieger, J. E., & Hu, W. (2008). The broadband digital divide and the nexus of race, competition, and quality. *Information Economics and Policy, 20*(2), 150–167. https://doi.org/10.1016/j.infoecopol.2008.01.001

Ranker, J. (2006). "There's fire magic, electric magic, ice magic, or poison magic": The world of video games and Adrian's compositions about "Gauntlet Legends." *Language Arts, 84*(1), 21–33. https://www.jstor.org/stable/41962160

Reynolds, M. C. (1989). *Knowledge base for the beginning teacher.* Pergamon Press.

Rodríguez, L. J. (2005). *My nature is hunger: New & selected poems, 1989–2004.* Curbstone Press/Rattle Edition.

Rodriguez, T., Hallman, H. L., & Pastore-Capuana, K. (2020). *Invested stayers: How teachers thrive in challenging times.* Rowman & Littlefield.

Rogers, R., & Mosley, M. (2006, October/November/December). Racial literacy in a second-grade classroom: Critical race theory, Whiteness studies, and literacy research. *Reading Research Quarterly, 41* (4), 462-495. https://www.jstor.org/stable/4151814

Rose, C. (1993, October 7). *Charlie Rose Interviews Toni Morrison* [TV series episode]. Public Broadcasting Service.

Russell, M., Bebell, D., O'Dwyer, L., Duffany, K., & O'Connor, K. (2003). Examining teacher technology use. *Journal of Teacher Education, 54*(4), 297–310. https://doi.org/10.1177/0022487103255985

Sawyer, L. L. (2017). *"Don't try and play me out!": The performances and possibilities of digital Black womanhood* (Published dissertation). https://surface.syr.edu/etd.785

Schick, C. (2002). Keeping the ivory tower white: Discourses of racial domination. In S. H. Razack (Ed.), *Race, space, and the law: Unmapping a White settler society* (pp. 99–119). Between the Lines.

Schultz, K. (2002). Looking across space and time: Reconceptualizing literacy learning in and out of school. *Research in the Teaching of English, 36*(3), 356–390. https://www.jstor. org/stable/40171531

Sealey-Ruiz, Y. (2011). Learning to talk and write about race: Developing racial literacy in a college English classroom. *English Quarterly: Journal of The Canadian Council of Teachers of English Language Arts, 42*(1), 24–42.

Sealey-Ruiz, Y. (2013). Toward a pedagogy of racial literacy in first-year composition. *Teaching English in the Two-Year College (TETYC), 40,* 384–398.

Sealey-Ruiz, Y. (2020). *The racial literacy development model.* Retrieved from https://www.yolandasealeyruiz.com/archaeology-of-self

Sealey-Ruiz, Y. (in press). The critical literacy of race: Toward racial literacy in teacher education. In H. R. Milner & K. Lomotey (Eds.), *Handbook of urban education* (2nd ed.). Routledge.

Sealey-Ruiz, Y., & Greene, P. (2015). Popular visual images and the (mis)reading of Black male youth: A case for racial literacy in urban preservice teacher education. *The International Journal of Teaching Education, 26*(1), 55–76. https://doi.org/10.1080/10476210.2014.997702

Sealey-Ruiz, Y., & Greene, P. (2011). Embracing urban youth culture in the context of education. *The Urban Review, 43,* 339–357. doi:10.1007/s11256-010-0156-8

Seglem, R., & Garcia, A. (2015). "So we have to teach them or what?": Introducing preservice teachers to the figured worlds of urban youth through digital conversation. *Teachers College Record, 117*(3).

Skerrett, A. (2011). English teachers' racial literacy knowledge and practice. *Race Ethnicity and Education, 14*(3), 313–330. https://doi.org/10.1080/13613324.2010.543391

Sleeter, C. E. (2001). Preparing teachers for culturally diverse schools: Research and the overwhelming presence of Whiteness. *Journal of Teacher Education, 52*(2), 94–106. https://doi.org/10.1177/0022487101052002002

Sleeter, C. E. (2017). Critical race theory and the Whiteness of teacher education. *Urban Education, 52*(2), 155–169. https://doi.org/10.1177/0042085916668957

Stevenson, H. C. (2014). *Promoting racial literacy in schools: Differences that make a difference.* Teachers College Press.

Stobaugh, R. R., & Tassell, J. L. (2011). Analyzing the degree of technology use occurring in pre-service teacher education. *Educational Assessment, Evaluation and Accountability, 23* (2), 143–157.

Sue, D. W., Capodilupo, C. M., Torino, G. C., Bucceri, J. M., Holder, A. M. B., Nadal, K. L., & Esquilin, M. (2007). Racial microaggressions in everyday life: Implications for clinical practice. *American Psychologist, 62*(4), 271–286. https://doi.org/10.1037/0003-066X.62.4.271

Tatum, B. D. (1997). *Why are all the Black kids sitting together in the cafeteria? and other conversations about race.* Perseus Books.

Terrill, M., & Mark, D. (2000). Preservice teachers' expectations for schools with children of color and second-language learners. *Journal of Teacher Education, 51*(2), 149–155. https://doi.org/10.1177/002248710005100209

Twine, W. F. (2003). Racial literacy in Britain: Antiracist projects, Black children and White parents. *Contours: A Journal of the African Diaspora, 1*(2), 129–153. https://doi.org/10.1080/0141987042000268512

Twine, W. F. (2010). *A white side of black Britain: Interracial intimacy and racial literacy.* Duke University Press.

Vandebosch, H., & Van Cleemput, K. W. (2008). Defining cyberbullying: A qualitative research into the perceptions of youngsters. *CyberPsychology and Behavior, 11*(4), 499–503. https://doi.org/10.1089/cpb.2007.0042

Vasquez, V. M. (2014). *Negotiating critical literacies with young children.* Routledge.

Vasquez, V. M., & Felderman, C. B. (2013). *Technology and critical literacy in early childhood.* Routledge.

Vasudevan, L. (2006). Making known differently: Engaging visual modalities as spaces to author new selves. *E-Learning and Digital Media, 3*(2), 207–216. https://doi.org/10.2304/elea.2006.3.2.207

Vasudevan, L. (2010). Literacies in a participatory, multimodal world: The arts and aesthetics of Web 2.0. *Language Arts, 88*(1), 43.

Vasudevan, L., Schultz, K., & Bateman, J. (2010). Rethinking composing in a digital age: Authoring literate identities through multimodal storytelling. *Written Communication, 27*(4), 442–468. https://doi.org/10.1177/0741088310378217

Völlink, T., Bolman, A. W. C., Dehue, F., & Jacobs, C. L. N. (2013). Coping with cyberbullying: Differences between victims, bully-victims and children not involved in bullying. *Journal of Community and Applied Social Psychology, 23*(1), 7–24. https://doi.org/10.1002/casp.2142

Webb-Johnson, G. C., & Carter, N. (2007, Summer). Culturally responsive urban school leadership: Partnering to improve outcomes for African American learners. *The National Journal of Urban Education and Practice, 1*(1), 77–99.

Wohlwend, K. E. (2009). Early adopters: Playing new literacies and pretending new technologies in print-centric classrooms. *Journal of Early Childhood Literacy, 9*(2), 117–140.

Wright, V. H., & Wilson, E. K. (2011). Teachers' use of technology: Lessons learned from the teacher education program to the classroom. *SRATE Journal, 20*(2), 48–60.

Zeichner, K. (1993). Connecting genuine teacher development to the struggle for social justice. *Journal of Education for Teaching, 19*(1), 5–20. https://doi.org/10.1080/0260747930190102

Zumwalt, K., & Craig, E. (2008). Who is teaching? Does it matter? In M. Cochran-Smith, S. Feiman-Nemser & D. J. McIntyre (Eds.), *Handbook of research on teacher education: Enduring questions in changing contexts* (pp. 404–423). Routledge.

Index

About the Authors

Dr. Detra Price-Dennis is an award-winning associate professor of education in the Department of Mathematics, Science, and Technology at Teachers College, Columbia University, in the Communications, Media, Learning Technologies, and Design program. Detra serves as co-director of the Reimagining Education Online Advanced Certificate Program, and is the founding director of #JustLit, a media-based project that seeks to provide multimodal resources about literature, media, and social change in education. Her scholarship draws on ethnographic and sociocultural lenses to examine the intersections of literacy education, technology, and curriculum development as means to identify and amplify equity-oriented pedagogies in K–8 classrooms. Please visit her at detrapricedennis.com or follow her on Twitter @ detramichelle.

Dr. Yolanda Sealey-Ruiz is an award-winning associate professor in English education at Teachers College, Columbia University. Her research focuses on racial literacy in teacher education, Black girl literacies, and Black and Latinx male high school students. A sought-after speaker on issues of race, culturally responsive pedagogy, and diversity, Sealey-Ruiz works with K–12 and higher-education school communities to increase their racial literacy knowledge and move toward more equitable school experiences for their Black and Latinx students. Sealey-Ruiz appeared in Spike Lee's *2 Fists Up: We Gon' Be Alright*, a documentary about the Black Lives Matter movement and the campus protests at Mizzou. She is the coeditor of three books and has authored several academic publications. Her first full-length book of poetry, *Love from the Vortex & Other Poems*, engages her theory of Archaeology of Self around the topics of love and intimacy. The book was published in March 2020 by Kaleidoscope Vibrations. Yolanda's sophomore poetry book, *The Peace Chronicles*, will be released in 2021. Please visit with her at yolandasealeyruiz.com, @RuizSealey on Twitter, and @yolie_sealeyruiz on Instagram.